Suzanne Scafe was born in Kingston, Jamaica, in 1954. After taking a post-graduate degree at the University of London Institute of Education she taught for three years at a secondary school in Jamaica. She was co-ordinator of a supplementary school in Brixton and is currently a lecturer at the Brixton College for Further Education. She is also one of the three authors of *The Heart of the Race: Black Women's Lives in Britain* (Virago, 1985).

In *Teaching Black Literature* Suzanne Scafe examines the role of literature in a multicultural curriculum and argues that for the text to be valued, it cannot simply be a matter of introducing a few Black texts in what is little more than a tokenistic gesture. This becomes for Black students an experience of being patronised by the school, the curriculum and the teachers. She stresses how crucial the task is for educationalists to ensure that Black writing is valued critically; that it is read both as a cultural and artistic whole and as a reflection of the political and cultural struggles that give it its context.

Teaching
Black Literature

Suzanne Scafe

VIRAGO

Published by VIRAGO PRESS Limited 1989
20–23 Mandela Street, Camden Town, London NW1 0HQ

Copyright © Suzanne Scafe 1989

A CIP catalogue for this book is
available from the British Library

Typeset in Great Britain by
Butler & Tanner Ltd, Frome and London

Printed by Cox & Wyman Ltd, Reading, Berkshire

Contents

Acknowledgements

Thank you to all the students who agreed to be interviewed; to Kehinde in particular, Jumoke, and all the students in FCC 1.

Many thanks to Jane Miller for her interest and encouragement: to Jan McKenley for her advice and support and to Yvette.

Introduction

Most students at schools or colleges in inner-city areas have had some encounters with Black literary texts. It may be a poem, a short story, a song or an extract from a novel. The struggle of teachers, parents and students in the past to introduce these texts into a literature curriculum has been long and hard. Opposition from the defenders of educational institutions whose role is to perpetrate particular, selective cultural forms, representing the cultural production of a minority elite, has been formidable. There has been reluctance too on the part of those who see the teaching of literature in schools as part of the process of establishing and confirming a 'literary tradition'.

The section of the Kingman Report entitled 'Language in relation to aesthetic development' voices the concerns of those who have regarded with some scepticism attempts to change either approaches to teaching the English curriculum, or its content. It criticises what is perceived as a tendency to emphasise the 'relevant' and to use literature as a 'setting for vigorous moral and social discussion'. The result, according to the report, is that teachers ignore the literary style of a text and its contribution to students' own understanding of language. A clear warning is issued:

> It is possible that a generation of children may grow up deprived of their entitlement – an introduction to the powerful and splendid history of the best that has been thought and said in our language. Too rigid a concern

with what is 'relevant' to the lives of young people seems to pose the danger of impoverishing not only the young people, but the culture itself, which has to be revitalised by each generation. (Committee of Inquiry into the Teaching of English language, 1988. p.11)

The problems of introducing Black literature into an English syllabus are further compounded by the liberal intentions of those who feel that it is enough for Black students, the students for whom they intend these texts, to have some interaction with cultural forms with which they can 'identify'. Texts are used in a tokenistic way and it is assumed that one or two examples of Black literature on a predominantly white male, middle-class syllabus can change the whole system of social and political relations which operate within and outside the schools to under-mine Black students' potential and make them feel culturally inadequate.

Students read texts in classrooms and seminar rooms in the context of such conflicting ideology. In many cases, the experience they have of reading the text is not a positive one, and for younger students it is not easy to identify why this is so. The experience either slips out of memory or becomes part of a general feeling of being patronised by the school, the curriculum and the teachers. To identify why the strategies adopted have been inadequate requires an outline of the historical processes that determined them. It is necessary to look at the early initiatives which gave rise to the change from a monocultural approach to teaching to a multicultural approach in order to understand how, both ideologically and practically, the strategies for change adopted within areas of the education system were flawed.

English lessons have, perhaps, been the site for the most concerted attempts to operate a multicultural curriculum. Literature is used to illustrate linguistic and cultural diversity; it is also used to illuminate social problems. It is the latter use which has been the most controversial and it is for this reason that reports such as the Kingman Report are persuasive. Parents, students and Black teachers particularly are concerned that the literature is being used to represent a culture which they neither identify with nor recognise. It is felt that teachers use literature in an undiscriminating way, with the result that stereotypic images are reinforced rather than challenged.

It is important to guard against a retreat of the kind expressed in the Kingman Report and to stress the value to all students of an English curriculum which is culturally diverse and receptive to change and innovation. Effective change, however, cannot be made without the development of a theoretical context for an approach to literature which is neither 'selective' nor exclusive; and which does not devalue the experience and literary production of the culture of the majority of students who are reading literature in an educational context. The theoretical base which gives rise to a notion of 'tradition' which is outside lived experience, needs to be challenged, so that 'reading' becomes an activity which includes rather than excludes the history and experiences of readers, writers and texts.

I began with an idea that Black literature was not being valued in schools and colleges and was influenced initially by studies which argued against a socio-literary approach to reading it. As I listened to the responses of students, however, and thought carefully about my own experiences of teaching and being taught Black literature, it became clear that I had been using value to mean status as well and that by so doing I was beginning a process of further alienating the majority of students from these texts. I came to the conclusion that a far more radical approach was needed than one which merely argued for a parallel canon of Black literary works. The whole white, male, literary tradition and the criteria by which texts enter that tradition had to be challenged.

Since many of the students I encounter read Black literature as stimulus material in their language lessons, I have begun by looking at the use of such texts in a multicultural curriculum and at the role of Black literature in encouraging students' awareness of different language forms and functions. The final section of the book is concerned with the development of a theoretical position which begins to look at Black literature in relation to other literature, which recognises its difference and examines ways in which that difference can be constructively exploited.

Because I felt that I needed to develop my argument within a framework whose terms of reference were containable, I have referred in detail to literature from the Caribbean, Africa and America. The term 'Black', however, is used throughout in its broadest, political sense.

1

Teacher as Learner

Fourteen years ago, one of the major factors in my decision to choose a new and supposedly 'progressive' university was that it offered, amongst its range of courses an option to study Black American literature and history. I expected, perhaps naively, that we would explore authors such as Baldwin who, it had seemed, had spoken 'personally' to me at fifteen about growing up Black in a white society. He had spoken about the church: its stifling power, the guilt and shame it engenders in the innocent; about Black families, mothers and fathers and sons; about the tensions created between white people and Black people struggling for power; about the personal trauma experienced by Black people trying to determine their own lives. I was confident that I'd be given new insights and that reading in the context of university seminars would enrich and broaden the experiences that had been profoundly, and emotionally, moving.

What happened, of course, was that the experience that I'd had of reading about Black lives – not Othello or other heroic figures of a white consciousness and a racist culture, but as they're lived – was shattered by the tools of literary criticism and a hostile literary establishment. There was something devastating about seeing or listening to texts in which I felt implicated, destroyed by the dry cutting tones of an English seminar. And in those grey bare rooms bright young lecturers were establishing careers for themselves commuting across the Atlantic, pronouncing as experts on 'my' history, culture and its cultural production. Our vulnerability (there were two of us) as young, alienated Black students, who did not have the brittle confidence others had acquired in public schools, was exploited. We were expected to attend and even to confer credibility on these dubious proceedings and to make a contribution which could then be described as emotional or subjective. Our only defence was to change, to dull our sensibilities – and therefore our responses – to suit the more objective, intellectual approach required by academia.

I lost more than I gained but somehow I got through in one piece by becoming distanced from the writers with whom I had so intensely identified. I became conscious of their 'outsider' status and aware only of how their works illuminated the 'Negro' or 'Black Problem' or gave insights into the life of the ghetto. I was able to remember, never to forget, the 'music' of *Othello* but needed to rediscover later, again by myself, Baldwin's rich lyricism, the description of a soul in torment, which I had then described as 'hysteria'. I was not given the tools to explore the 'universality' of writers such as Hansberry, Jones (Baraka), Toomer, McKay and the 'truths' contained in the texts. I was even less equipped to understand the jazz poets – Ted Joans, etc. – whose do-wop rhythms were withering and dying in such a barren, alienating environment. As he read his poems, the more established lecturers greeted the reading with cool incomprehension or even with a patronising nod, while the students flushed with embarrassed excitement. Was this literature or could it ever be? Was it pop-art, jazz? Was it even art?

Some years after I had been a student in an all-white institution, I became a teacher in a college in South London. Although all the students there are Black, they are taught language and literature by predominantly white lecturers, in an organisation until recently managed almost entirely by white staff. I am aware of some of the contradictions students have to face and resolve, unsupported, when they are asked to read Black writers in the classroom context. While I am not proposing to look in detail at the literature of GCSE and A level courses nor of degree syllabuses, I am concerned with the way the cultural and educational principles, learnt and internalised by teachers, both inform literature teaching at examination level and determine what literature is taught to the great majority of students who do not sit a literature examination. As a reader and a teacher I am also concerned to foster in students an interest in and a critical respect for literature of the Black diaspora. I recognise, however, that some of the ambivalent or even antagonistic feelings students have towards Black literature are the result of the inculcation of these literary values by educational institutions.

The range of responses I have encountered in both traditional, statutory institutions and non-traditional establishments, though diverse, have all had striking similarities. They have all been, either consciously or unconsciously, extremely complex, and sometimes within one response there have been stark contradictions. The supplementary school where I taught full-time was committed to using Black literature and to displaying Black cultural and historical images. The majority of students who were taught at the school were at early secondary level and did not, on the whole, resist the literature used in the classroom. Often, they did express feelings that it was significantly relevant to their experience, and as a result they were frequently overwhelmed by its seriousness and by some of the demands both the writing itself, and the teachers, were making of them. One student, for example, became very angry and distressed after reading 'Frankie Mae', a short story about a girl with the potential to achieve so much, but whose life had become shattered by the systematic abuse of herself and her father by the white landowners. It was indeed her brightness and perceptiveness which had made Frankie Mae and her family the victims of the landowners' hatred. The student struggled with the text and after asking 'Are you trying to make me hate white

people?' wanted to leave the room. In this case, because of
the powerful connections with her own experiences, she felt
encroached upon by the teacher and made vulnerable by feelings
which were as yet fully unexplored and unresolved. She felt
she could leave the group, justifying this on the grounds that
we really should not have been studying these texts at all. The
texts they expected to read and discuss were ones from which
they felt comfortably distanced. (There was, in addition, nothing
in 'Frankie Mae' which signalled that it was either 'English' or
'Literature', and the process of reading it was further com-
plicated by the fact that it was taught in a Black school.) If in
a traditional educational institution the connections between
Black literature and a school English curriculum are not made,
students will retain that sense of separation and distinction.

At most London Further Education Colleges there are students who want to read Black literature and learn about its
history. In addition, there are some students who either tolerate
these subjects as examples of the many liberal teaching strategies
which come and go, or those who associate its inclusion in the
English curriculum with failure. After teaching at a Further
Education College for some months I had formed some idea of
why students felt that way. Many teachers use Black writing in
English classes because they feel that they ought to, since 90
per cent of the college students are Black. Our language policy
stresses the need for teachers to use material which reflects the
students' cultural background, and there is a wide range of
possible literature available. Many, however, feel threatened by
the ideological content of some of the texts, and vulnerable to –
even targets for – students' hostility. This lack of confidence in
their use of the material leads to mistrust by the students:
of the lecturer, the interaction they are being asked to participate
in and the text itself. Students, who are used to taking their
cues from the teacher, often find that they are being expected
to take the initiative in responding to descriptions of racism and
oppression or of discrimination within their culture, to moments

of humour they never expected to see represented in a class-room, and to the text's overall relevance to their own lives. Students who cannot easily take up positions of openness about aspects of their lives which they have never been able or even desired to express in school become suspicious and feel manipulated.

Literacy and Special Educational Needs classes draw heavily on Black material, and the walls of their rooms are usually covered with displays of examples of Black culture. Yet this thrust is not reflected in the English Literature syllabus – for example, where a Black text has never been studied as a set book. The college regularly invites Black poets, performers and so on, and the audience consists of teachers, who bring along students who are often pursuing neither academic nor vocational courses. English and Communication is a part of every course. The majority of students on 'serious' courses do not attend, even though the performances are scheduled during class time and are therefore categorised, in terms of the institution, as 'educational'. None of the performances is discussed or contextualised educationally before or after the performance, so I imagine that the college audience feels that they are there purely to be entertained. If the work of these performers and poets – L. K. Johnson, Mickey Smith – appears in the classroom again, and without any kind of context, it is not surprising that the students wonder about its subtext, and conclude that they are being delivered 'diversionary' material.

What follows is an extract from a conversation between myself and two literature students, Jumoke and Kehinde. I had taught them literature for a term before I interviewed them, and I chose to do so because I knew that they held conflicting views. In some ways they represented a polarisation of possible responses, though they were also expressing individual views. The discussion echoes those which took place twenty years ago, and

Kehinde articulates demands that were being made as many years ago by students who are now her teachers. The changes, these students seem to suggest, are merely cosmetic. There is as well a certain scepticism about motives for teaching Black literature, and a wariness that the way it gets taught might undermine some of the benefits of its inclusion in the curriculum.

Both students are in my O level Literature group. I have come to know Kehinde very well and we have had many conversations of the kind that I have taped. I know Jumoke less well, but I feel that she expresses the disappointment and hostility some students feel towards a multicultural or anti-racist curriculum. The students' conversation encapsulates two general questions I want to address in this book. First, if Black literature is to be taught in schools, how can we avoid students' rejection of its importance as part of the curriculum? Secondly – and to take Kehinde's point – what is meant by a 'political' reading of literature? Is this a reading which is particular to Black texts and is there a disjunction between a 'political' and an 'aesthetic' response to literature?

SUZANNE: Would you like to study some of these books at college?

JUMOKE: We did already. Well, not books but things about Black people. I get fed up with it really. I didn't really come to college for that. Some of it's all right yeah.

KEHINDE: I would, yeah. You didn't get fed up with all the white books you read in school though, did you? All my life I've been reading white books, and a lot of them are racist but Black books are forgotten, like they don't exist. Black literature plays an important part in our lives. There are Black people in society and reading Black books would teach more people to be aware. You imagine that the world was made by white people and we're just here. Black literature plays an important part in our education.

JUMOKE: Yeah, yeah. That's right. The thing is, though, it doesn't get you anywhere, does it? I mean we listened to music and we did some of those poets. It's not really English though, is it? I've never seen an exam in it anyway.

KEHINDE: Well I'd still do it even if it didn't lead to an exam. I've never studied Linton Kwesi Johnson and we could study him. His way of writing's different.

SUZANNE: What do you mean?

KEHINDE: I mean like Linton writes about Black people and the police and we're here to stay and all that. It's political isn't it? That's what is important.

JUMOKE: I'm not interested in politics – y'know what I mean.

KEHINDE: But anything, love or old people like those poems we did about English old people. Black people do write about love and that but not in the same wording. We could talk about being old but in a different way: remembering the village or wanting to go back, not just growing old in a block of flats. We see things differently, y'know what I mean? White people identify white interests. Take comedy, with comedy, white comedy's different, the humour's different. The novels and poems and whatever don't have to be political, it can be like your own experience, anything. A Black way of living but set in a way that a Black person can identify with. Not about some white middle-class place in the country you know?

SUZANNE: So what made you decide to study English Literature?

KEHINDE: English literature? I dunno. I dunno why I'm doing it. I wanted to do Black history really. I want to know more Black history but it wouldn't be recognised in the exam.

SUZANNE: And Black literature?

KEHINDE: Yeah. We should read a lot of Black literature and we should do it with Black teachers.

SUZANNE: Have you been taught by Black teachers before – at school?

KEHINDE: No, no. I was in a white school and then it sort of changed when the Blacks got there. In Islington, they said it went downhill when the Blacks came [laughs] but then it changed back. There were never more Blacks than whites anyway. I don't want white teachers teaching me about Black people anyway. You should go about learning your own way. You should learn yourselves by teaching yourselves. They go to the West Indies and Africa, teaching us about ourselves, but they'd teach us in a way that would control us. Even some Black people with a Black background are not aware, but white people can't not be racist; they can be less racist but those that think they aren't fail to recognise their racism. Like they say racist things without realising it. Like the Black sections, what do you think about Black sections? It's like F— said that they're a form of apartheid ... With the African novels a lot of it is to do with me – my culture. I feel it's more interesting than white literature – I've got more in common with it ... it's about village life and ordinary things like a belief in God. Their religious beliefs are more related to their everyday life and different to the Christian belief that's drummed into my head. I think Christianity is alienating [laughs]. Yes it's alienating. Oh yeah ... we did *Black Boy* and *Second Class Citizen* last year. *Black Boy* was about this boy and his mum

hustling to earn a living and that. He creates a picture of what really did
happen and you feel more emotional about his experience.

Kehinde explains that she wants to study Black literature
because it is an important part of her experience and in turn
an important part of her discovery of herself, which needs to be
developed, explored and used to counter the dominance of
cultural forms and practices from which she feels alienated. It
would seem, however, that within the limitations of a traditional
study of 'literature', there is no room for responses which draw
on and relate to readers' experience and are important precisely
for that reason.

There is the need, as the discussion illustrates, to retread
some of the old ground and to re-examine the multi-cultural
debate, in order to discover why students feel compromised and
resentful. This is so even though, in theory at least, some of the
demands for changes in the curriculum to represent the cultures
of growing numbers of Black children in British schools have
been met. As teachers committed to dismantling a racist, culturally biased approach to literature teaching, we need to build
strategies which do not undermine students' sense of themselves
and of their place within social and cultural communities. If we
are going to teach Black literature to Black and white students,
the teaching must confirm the importance of the texts as part
of the whole school or college curriculum.

2

Literature, Culture and Multiculturalism

Groups within the Black community have been mobilising to improve the educational offer to Black children since the early sixties, when significant numbers of Caribbean children began to enter the British school system, their parents having come here in the 1950s and 1960s as workers. It is commonly supposed that Caribbean parents had no understanding of the British school system and therefore assumed that their children were receiving a sound education. If they weren't, it was thought, the parents lacked the skills and confidence to enter the schools and press for change. The children were left, therefore, to suffer at the hands of racist teachers in a school system which denied them access to a successful education, devalued or ignored their culture and histories and generally assumed that they were below average intelligence. However, what little documentation there is, shows that Black pupils' underachievement in schools was not passively accepted by parents. Black workers in factories, service industries and public services saw the racism with which they were confronted daily mirrored in schools, and they extended the brief of their workers' organisations to encompass educational issues.

As early as 1965–6, members of the North London West Indian Association were organising to alert parents to the fact that 70 per cent of Black children were in ESN schools, and later to protest against the banding of primary-school leavers.

The strategies which they adopted to counteract such dangerous trends indicated that they felt it was the racism in schools which was responsible for this labelling. They felt that the establishment of all Black organisations such as youth clubs and all Black Supplementary Schools would provide students with some understanding of their history and culture and give them the confidence to assert their case in the face of the damaging onslaught of negative images they encountered in schools. They also wanted to enable students to achieve a sound education, and to equip them with the basic skills needed for successful participation in the community. By the early 1970s Supplementary Schools were established all over London and in other cities where there were Caribbean communities. The main objective of these schools – and many of them have survived and grown more successful – is to supplement or to correct mainstream schools' mis-education of Black children. The schools teach traditional syllabuses, often using traditional methods, but the difference between Supplementary Schools and a 'traditional' education in British schools or a remembered colonial education is that teachers in the smaller, more personalised context of supplementary-schools classrooms do not expect pupils to fail or to underachieve. The teachers, who are mainly Black, consciously seek ways of inspiring confidence in the children's ability to achieve. The curriculum, primarily core subjects, is taught alongside or as part of programmes of cultural awareness, and the names of even the very earliest schools – George Padmore, Albertina Sylvester, Kwame Nkrumah (all established in North London in 1970) reflect this emphasis.

A pamphlet published by the Croydon Black Parents Committee in the early seventies illustrates the concern of parents at this neglect and draws attention to the correlation between knowledge and belief in self, cultural pride, and academic and social achievement:

There are other areas of importance where you can help your child. A lot of what they teach Black children gives them bad impressions of themselves, often the books they read talk about savages. The result is they become ashamed of themselves and Black people in general for being black ... teach them to be proud of themselves. Tell them about the land of their birth [the West Indies, etc.] and about our ancestral home in Africa ...

Education is of the greatest importance for us as a community. If we think about the problems now and do something about it, Black people may have a chance and a future in this country.

Although some schools in the London boroughs have attempted to redress this cultural imbalance, Supplementary Schools still emphasise cultural awareness, often expressing the opinion that the transmission of Black culture in an educational context is safer in the hands of Black educators outside the school system than with misinformed white teachers within it.

In the early 1970s Black students and teachers were also pressing for change. Students at Tulse Hill School, for example, who wanted to turn the notion of social and cultural deprivation on its head, initiated the demand for Black Studies. An account of the way in which the agenda of a Black Studies course was hijacked by white teachers within the school is instructive. It mirrors the same processes of change and absorption which have taken place in London generally, where early demands from the Black community, though receiving official commitment from educational institutions, are still a long way from realisation.

The Tulse Hill students won the right to organise a Black Studies programme, to determine its objectives and to decide which speakers would be invited to talk about subjects specified by the students themselves. Because of the success of the programme and, possibily, because of its threat to the authority and control of the school, the teachers within the school sought to incorporate Black Studies into the main curriculum and so advise students on what issues were selected for attention. The students, recognising that their hard-won battles to determine for themselves what needed to be taught were about to be appropriated to suit the school establishment, insisted that the teachers relinquish their power within the institution and allow them to organise their study groups as they had originally determined. The teachers conceded: some felt displaced and confused at the rejection of what they had considered to be a positive intervention.

There may be other less well-documented examples of students intervening successfully in the school curriculum. However, without the support of an organised group of Black students articulating their dissatisfaction or even constructively identifying its cause Black students in schools all over Britain have tended to opt out, making a clear statement, by their refusal, that the schools have failed to offer them any real future within this society.

The absence of Black teachers as a potential pool of support clearly compounded the problem. Those who were teaching in British schools at that time felt isolated and unsupported. Their contribution was regarded with suspicion and attempts to revise an obviously racist, substandard curriculum were often met with hostility.

Mariana Maxwell, a Black teacher teaching in North London during the late 1960s, writes describing her anger and frustration at being asked to contain students and to stifle their aspirations, so that the students are concerned only with survival, while drawing the least possible amount of attention to themselves. She comments:

> But why should anybody worry too much, the kids are only a bunch of Blacks to be managed and screamed at like animals, or a bunch of white kids too poor to be bothered with too much anyway. All of them are going to be porters or hairdressers so what? was the comment one grey morning. The use of films is widespread. It is much easier to show films than to try to teach.   (Dhondy *et al.*, 1982, p. 24)

An analogy in a late eighties context could be made with the use of Black literature. Teachers can use the material in an attempt to divert students' attention away from the educationally and intellectually bankrupt offer schools and colleges make to students on non-certificated courses. It is also used in the hope that students will be entertained and be occupied for the length of the lesson. Farouk Dhondy (1982) questions his own objectives when teaching Black literature in schools. He describes the complex interaction between students and teacher when attempting to teach literature which represents the language and culture of the Caribbean. When the school sanctions these methods of teaching and these curriculum changes, does it presume that students' expectations of their own education will, as a result, be more nearly realised? He concludes:

> School will still produce a small percentage of skilled workers, a large percentage of unskilled ones. I will have kept the last category busy, motivated and believing that I am somehow on their side because I know the facts about slavery. (Dhondy *et al.*, 1982, p. 19)

Bernard Coard's work consolidated the demands from various groups within the Black community for a better education for Black children. It articulated the need for change in both the curriculum and in teachers' attitudes. He condemns the schools for excluding Black history and culture from the curriculum, describing this exclusion as 'criminal negligence'. He argues too that the students have absorbed the negative self-images perpetuated by the school and other state institutions in relation to Black culture and cultural forms. He blames the negative characterisations of the culture for behavioural problems in some students and for a certain neurosis about their self-image in relation to white culture. If Black people are not represented as grotesque caricatures then they are ignored and it is as if – as Kehinde confirms in an earlier interview – white people construct the world and are the makers and doers, the creators of culture and societies, and 'we're just here'.

A succession of government reports has registered alarm at the disruption in schools identified with Black students. They have been concerned too about the growing rate of juvenile

crime and have linked disaffection and failure at school with the
trend towards crime and violence. The containment strategies
were clearly failing, and educationalists were being asked to
reconsider the offer made by schools and colleges and to investigate ways of motivating students to stay on in schools. State
intervention on the issue of curriculum changes to meet the
needs of Black students began with consideration of the model
of 'compensatory education', in operation in inner-city schools
in America. These were based on a deficit model of Black
working-class students' cultural environment. Teachers here
preferred a less obviously discriminatory approach – multi-
culturalism, which sought to value equally all students'
culture – and urged that the diversity of their cultures be
represented in classrooms. More recently, the strategies pro-
posed by the more progressive education authorities have been
'anti-racist' ones, where teachers are encouraged to incorporate
into their teaching practice an analysis of the political, historical
and cultural processes which have given rise to present inequalities and discriminatory practices.

Clearly these approaches, even the least threatening, have
been adopted less than enthusiastically by most schools and
colleges, and where they have been adopted it is generally as
piecemeal solutions to problems of control. They do not challenge either the school system, the culture and ethos of the
schools, or the ideology which informs the curriculum. As a
result, Black parents, teachers and pupils blame these strategies
for diverting attention away from the real problems of a discriminatory school system. 'Multiracial education' is identified
by Black educationalists such as Maureen Stone (1981) as
actively compounding the mis-education of Black students.

Stone would further argue that attempts by teachers to com-
pensate for Black students' lack of positive self-image and cultural identity are, in fact, racist. Their culture, she states, is
intact, but students recognise that it has no place in schools.
From the students' point of view, to bring representations of

their culture such as 'dialect' into schools would dilute its oppositional role; it would allow teachers entry into a way of speaking which is used to subvert, and is powerful precisely because it is seen by students to have no legitimacy in schools.

If as a teacher one is committed to change in the curriculum and to using Black literature as a tool for change in the curriculum as a whole and not as an optional form of entertainment for those who, it is supposed, cannot manage 'serious' literature, their arguments which endorse separation between the culture of schools and students' culture cannot be acceptable.

What has been described is a process whereby the methods of control by which initiatives for change are implemented move from the potential beneficiaries of those changes to the representatives of those in power within schools. The original objectives of a curriculum which included the study of Black history and culture have been redefined to the point where none of those original objectives has been met. Students do not appear to be more confident in their understanding of their cultural identity; neither has their performance significantly improved.

Schools have traditionally assumed the role of transmitting the cultural values of white middle-class Britain. Bourdieu (1976) argues that the dominant culture retains its dominance through its validation and transmission of specific practices and values in the schools. In order for this process to be effective, the context and character of a school's education must define themselves in terms of the dominant culture.

Lord Joseph, during his term as Secretary of State for Education, restated a commitment to ensuring that schools help students towards

an understanding of the intellectual, cultural, technological and political growth of the UK and the effects of these developments on the lives of its citizens.   (in Gundara, Jagdish (ed.), 1986, p. 116)

In order to acquire a successful education, it is still considered necessary for Black and working-class students to leave behind

the cultural environment of the home and the peer group and
to assimilate those of schools and of the schooled professional
classes.

The processes of transmission exclude the majority of
students, whose culture is either unrecognised or undermined.
An understanding of the role of educational institutions in
confirming the status of an elitist culture is important; it is also
important to recognise those systems which in practice exclude
and devalue, even if in theory their stated objectives are the
opposite. There is, however, a tendency among teachers to
underestimate the capacity of schools and society as a whole to
dissolve opposition. This becomes a failure to recognize the
ability of the school culture to absorb alternatives and successfully to oppose or change the existing culture. Stuart Hall
(1980) gives some indication of the complex structures which
transform oppositional strategies:

> One has to show that there are social and historical processes and that they
> are not written down in the stars, they are not handed down. They are
> deep conditions which are not going to change if we start tinkering around
> with them. We must not give our students that kind of illusion.
>
> (Hall, S., 1980, p. 6)

Bourdieu's analysis of these structures is useful in providing
an understanding of their complexity and interdependence.
He examines specifically the relationship between 'school' and
culture, arguing for a structuralist definition of culture as a
system of codes and formations which are established through
convention and which provide the structure and framework
within which new ideas, methods of analysis, and so on, are
formulated and expressed. A culture cannot be identified by its
products, its 'individual patterns', which change continuously
anyway, but must be understood as systems, 'master patterns',
which generate an infinite number of products. A culture is
above all defined by the forms of its expression rather by its
content. Thus culture, and in particular an academic culture, is

described as a common code expressing the same images, idioms, metaphors and particular rule-governed systems of thought, different in their individual expression but not in their essential structure.

If we were to apply Bourdieu's description of cultural patterns and codes which produce unified though sometimes seemingly dissenting practices to literary criticism, we would see that the central concepts of literature teaching, notions particularly of a 'personal response', are a chimera. Within an academic culture or 'school of thought' there are ways of responding which are personal, reflecting the style of the individual, but the response is still framed by a cultural system which limits and regulates it. There is concurrence even if the expression appears to represent conflict and disagreement. Thus, while there is an impression of freedom implicit in words such as 'criticism' and 'personal response', there are distinct guidelines or marked-out itineraries that the student has to follow.

These itineraries are, in fact, systems of discrimination. The divisions and distinctions which the school teaches students to observe reflect the social divisions in society which, to a large extent, the schools reinforce. In addition, as Gramsci illustrates, schools depoliticise intellectual thought and traditions and abstract their historical context. Overtly historical or political literature – or literature such as Black literature, whose expression seems explicitly political because of its form, its opposition to the codes and systems of 'traditional' European literature – is relegated to the margins of canonised literary texts.

There is, evidently, continual conflict between school culture and the culture of the students, and it is this area of conflict which needs to be exploited. In educational institutions, perhaps more than in any other social, political or economic institutions, the dominance of an elitist culture is contested, often by students and sometimes by teachers, who attempt to transform the content of the material they deliver into forms more relevant to students' lives and experience. However, Bourdieu's analysis emphasises the total integration of social and political institutions where structures are characterised as fixed, although their products or manifestations change.

In *Culture and Society* Raymond Williams argues, in relation to Leavis in this particular context, against the proposition that 'culture' has a fixed and absolute meaning, pointing out that the word has meant different things at different historical moments and will come to have different meanings while it is still in use. It is not an object or a package that people can acquire through training or example:

> The word culture cannot automatically be pressed into service as any kind of social or personal directive. Its emergence in its modern meanings marks the effort at total qualitative assessment, but what it indicates is a process not a conclusion.   (Williams, R., 1958, p. 285)

In his critique of an authoritative interpretation or method of interpretation, Williams says that meanings and values are determined by social and historical forces, since any interpretation is made in relation to experience and the context of its production. In 'Base and Superstructure in Marxist Cultural Theory', he describes the 'tradition' of literature as a selective one and argues that the ways in which it selects are not always direct and obvious. It is not simply a static ideology but active and changing sets of practices; it is the process of the dominant culture 'making and remaking' itself, in part through the incorporation of potentially threatening forms and practices. However, Williams defends the existence of a whole body of cultural production from groups whom the vanguards of 'taste and sensibility' have traditionally excluded, referred to in *Culture and Society* as 'proletarian', and later as 'oppositional'. The excluding nature of the dominant culture means that it does not incorporate the whole range of cultural practice. Certain forms intentionally challenge the dominant modes and the premise on which their dominance rests. They are thus by nature 'oppositional'.

Expressions of diverse cultural forms cannot be grafted on to an unchanged curriculum unless a historical and political context is provided for those forms. 'Black culture' is not a unified whole; if it exists, it is complex and contradictory and as vital as the ways of life which reflect it. Texts and cultural symbols cannot be introduced on the assumption that students will automatically identify with them and feel better for their entry into the classroom. Black students experience their relationship with a culture they define as 'Black' differently in different contexts. Sometimes they see it as a powerful, enabling tool; at other times they express rejection of it, feeling that their identification with certain forms and practices disenfranchises them from British society and prevents their success in it. Often they experience a mixture of the two.

The schools transmit, for example, the notion, passed off as truth, that culture is white, male and middle-class. This not only shapes Black students' expectations of the school, its purpose and function, but leads them to expect not to see aspects of their own culture and environment there. Yet as the interview with Jumoke and Kehinde illustrates, outside school, the cultural environment in which they function is self-affirming. Educationally, and ultimately socially and politically, however, it seems less important. The term 'cultural identity' is illusory. It suggests that there is an unproblematic and uncontested form, 'culture', that people identify with or reject in a straightforward way. Black students may identify with one cultural form and not another, or with one in certain contexts but not in others. Cultural symbols, literary texts which have not been fossilised in a 'tradition' – which is the case for most Black writing – may be particularly pertinent to the experiences of a community at one moment in history but not at another. The context of the interpretation may redefine a text which may have seemed liberating and celebratory at one moment in history and trite or idealistic at another. Cultural production cannot be automatically identified as meaningful to a student simply because both student and producer are Black. The schools' job is not to facilitate the process of standardising meaning and relevance.

In a lecture originally delivered on 20 February 1970 at Syracuse University, New York, Amilcar Cabral examines the role of culture in the struggle for liberation and its relationship to political movements. When speaking of African culture, he does not avoid contradictions and the disruption of safe mythology for the sake of political coherence and popular translation. He argues that the oppressor maintains domination by the 'permanent, organized repression of the cultural life of the people concerned'.

Using the example of his country's experience of Portuguese domination, he describes the denial by that colonial power of the existence of an African culture. He cites Salazar's assertion that 'Africa does not exist' as the epitome of the kind of arrogance and ignorance which are the manifestations of racism and cultural imperialism.

Africa, as a continent of diverse cultural communities under siege, has had to 'impose respect for cultural values' against such negative assertions. This, however, should not lead to a romanticising of the term 'culture'. It is not, he stresses, a uniform whole and he speaks of 'African cultures' – not 'an African culture' – which are the reflections of economic and political Africas.

Throughout his speeches there are references to an analogy between culture and a plant. The physical and material reality of a society are the roots of its history and culture. He describes culture as both an element of history and its product. It is the plant's flower, reflecting the history of a society and at the same time, generating and determining it. Culture represents the process by which a people in their day-to-day lives resist, resolve contradiction and survive; it is therefore the basis of historical progression. It is a dynamic process of adaptation and change and is not a definable 'body' but possesses characteristics which are both 'specific and unspecific':

> It is important not to lose sight of the fact that no culture is a perfect, finished whole. Culture, like history, is an expanding and developing phenomenon. Even more important, we must take account of the fact that the fundamental characteristic of a culture is the highly dependent and reciprocal nature of its linkages with the social and economic reality of the environment, with the level of productive forces and the mode of production of the society which created it.   (Cabral, A., 1973, p. 50)

Most Black students I encounter live in a cultural environment which is Black. They go to Black clubs, listen to Black music, socialise predominantly with Black peer groups, and so on. However, from time to time and sometimes frequently, students represent their 'Blackness' – their culture and themselves, in fact – in a negative or derogatory light. There is a sense in which the culture to which they relate provides some confidence, the potential for a group identity, a context for affirming self-worth; yet in relation to the wider, white community those same forms are perceived by the students as inferior.

To introduce Black literary texts into the classroom without being aware of some of the contradictions of a culture and its production, and some of the complex feelings students have in relation to it, creates problems. The potential the school may have to devalue the texts and their reading merely reinforces students' feelings about its otherness and may confirm their sense of the superiority of the dominant culture. Black literature as an oppositional cultural form cannot be taught alongside traditional literature in a way which leaves the cultural assumptions uncontested. It has to be used to question those assumptions, and in order to do this effectively Black literature must be taught in the context of a completely revised approach to English teaching. Black writing is often seen as an important part of the process of political liberation and is therefore contextualised by it. It presents a challenge in both its form – often the language used or the structure – and its content. It may not, however, always be read in that way, and a reading of such material in the classroom may, by virtue of its being there, negate its oppositional function. (As 'alternative' material it can either be read as unimportant or as a gesture on an O and A level syllabus, to which a student applies traditional methods of criticism.)

In practice, when the historical and political circumstances of the text's production are recognised, there is the tendency for the writing to be interpreted simply as a fictionalised representation and celebration of the struggle for liberation. In an article in *The English Magazine* entitled 'Reading and Race', Alvarado (1980), describing the fictional characterisations of Black literary production, writes:

> The imbalance of racial history ... means that black characters who actually do anything will often be active seekers of liberation from oppression, or people who have made it by conforming as closely as possible to white norms of behaviour ... (t)he fictional equivalents of Nyerere, Biko, Martin Luther King, Malcolm X, George Jackson, Mohammed Ali, Bob Marley ...   (p. 8)

The students are probably familiar with only one or two of these figures and they may or may not find it useful to identify with them. Most readers, in any case, would be hard put to find fictional equivalents of any of these figures in *Miguel Street*, *Things Fall Apart*, *Black Boy*, or *Friends*. These do not contain heroic representations. The strength of the characters is that they are complex and stand in contradictory relationships to either significant periods of history or to day-to-day experiences of life in a white or ex-colonial society. They therefore provide some common points of reference to students' own lives and experiences.

The whole article, which is a practical guide to the use of literature to alert students to and discuss with them issues of race, skirts around the cultural and literary implications of the task. It provides an example of the way in which oppositional cultures are oversimplified, and cultural forms such as Black writing are dismissed. To see Black literature as a rhetorical statement is to misunderstand completely the relationship between the writing and the circumstances of its production.

Approaches of this kind indicate the way in which attempts to diversify the curriculum can confirm its racist bias; as a result, more problems are created than solved. A reading of Black literature which identifies in the text role models for students to emulate will result in the separation of Black literature from other forms of literature on the curriculum. In this way, its potential to challenge the assumptions of the dominant culture is diffused. Black literature is seen as 'separate' and 'other' and placed firmly outside the mainstream of English writing.

If Black literature is to present a challenge to the cultural assumptions of English teaching, then as teachers we must not underestimate the system we are confronting – and its complexity. I think it is important to stress the capacity of the dominant culture to diffuse and divert struggle for change, and nowhere is this more apparent than in the attempt to move away from monocultural teaching, which is seen to ensure the failure of Black students, to a multicultural approach which in the experience of many Black students is no less alienating and certainly does not assist in their educational success. While stressing the capacity of the dominant culture to neutralise opposition, and by describing examples of instances where programmes for change have failed, I am not suggesting that failure is inevitable.

As a Black teacher I do think it is necessary to be able to see the potential for some dislocation of traditional assumptions. It is important that Black literature is taught in schools, but that it is taught in a way which does not confirm students' suspicions that it is 'substandard' and has no place there. This requires the development of a teaching strategy which recognises its difference and its power as a result of that difference. Its political significance cannot be ignored, nor should it be used to deny the literary value of Black texts. In order for English teachers to use Black literature to change the curriculum in a fundamental way, the political context of the texts and their difference need to be exploited and used to challenge the assumptions of current English teaching practices.

3

'It's like learning another language'

Myself and a group of eight students were huddled around one table reading Mikey Smith's poem 'Mi Cyaan Believe It'. The heating wasn't working, and one of the windows had either broken or couldn't be shut properly, so we all struggled to get some heat from a noisy fan heater.

We had had discussions about language just before Christmas, though I think that some members of this half of the group were not present at those lessons. We had looked at the formation of pidgin and Creole and examined the relationship between language and power. We were just getting into our stride when an incident occurred which powerfully illustrated for the students the racism of the British media and the way in which language is used to distort and misrepresent. Emblazoned on the front page of the *Sun* was the accusation in bold headlines that this group of students were 'racist', because they had taken a decision not to give a children's party to an all-white playgroup. On the day the headlines appeared telephone calls were made to the college by the National Front, and all the students were sent home at midday. Some weeks later an attempt was made to petrol-bomb the flat of the only other Black teacher on the course.

At first the students were relatively unperturbed by these incidents. The Black students in the group understand institutionalised racism: the report, the attack and the threats came as no surprise to them. They had sensed the hostility of the parents – confirmed by their reporting the story to both the right-wing local newspaper and to the *Sun* – and knew that their decision not to take their Caribbean folk songs, African and Indian children's stories and games to that environment had been the right one.

The two white students in the class were not so sure. They found it difficult to identify with the Black students in their judgements about the racism of the parents at the nursery, in the media, and in the college, where the teachers involved had displayed the usual reluctance actually to identify racism, preferring instead to look at ways of apportioning blame evenly.

By the end of February a clear split had formed between the Black students in the class and the two white students. One or two Black students were beginning to feel much less confident about their position and very uncomfortable about the open and growing hostility in the group. There was some tension in the group on the day we read the poem, and on reflection we should probably not have discussed 'Mi Cyaan Believe It' on that day. It would have been impossible to look at the poem as a discrete work, unassailable by outside influences. Inevitably, the anger contained in the poem fused with the students' recent experience to determine the kind of reading of the text which they produced. The lesson is instructive, however. It shows, importantly, that what was on the table that day was not just a poem in a variety of Standard English but a powerful statement about the historical and social context of language, and this needed to be addressed.

FIONA: Does anyone want to hear it, though? I can't take it.
SUZANNE: What do you mean? Do you understand it?
FIONA: Yeah, I understand it, but I can't see the point of it being like that.

The answer to Fiona's implied question, 'What's the point of writing like that?', is in part the meaning of the poem. Its intended effect is to shock and disturb ideas about poetry and writers and about the kind of language that gets written down. In that sense its meaning is in her question. The language of the poem speaks of the history of Creole, of the Caribbean and of its complex present-day relationship to Standard English within different social contexts. The language is, for the students, the most striking feature of the poem and their questions 'why' show their struggle to find out what the language symbolises.

While the poem is being read there is stirring, laughter, and the students draw attention to particular phrases. (I have asked someone to read).

PAT: Go on, Julie. You love it really, don't you?

Julie hesitates and mumbles. She does not feel very confident about reading. Her own language is a very uneasy mixture of Creole and Jamaican London and the other students often laugh at the way she speaks. It seems that her parents have tried to suppress her first language, Creole, and she is struggling to find a variety of Standard that is acceptable to both her parents and her peer group. Eventually she starts to read:

JULIE	OTHERS
Mi seh mi cyaan believe it	
mi seh mi cyaan believe it	cyaan believe
room dem a rent	it
mi apply widin	
but as mi go in	
cockroach rat an' scorpion also	
come in	[laughter]
waan good	
nose haffi run	
but me naw go siddung pan	
igh wall	igh wall
like Humpty Dumpty	[laughter]
mi a face me reality	
one lickle bwoy come blow im orn	blow im orn
an mi look pan im wid scorn	

an mi realize ow me five bwoy
pickney   pickney
was a victim of de tricks
dem call p ...

[SUZANNE: was a victim of de tricks dem call
partisan pally-trix]

                                                 ADEELA

an mi ban mi belly   an mi ban mi belly
an mi bawl   an mi bawl
                                                 [laughter]
an mi ban mi belly   an mi ban mi belly
an mi bawl   an mi bawl
lawd

                                                 CYNTHIA

mi cyaan believe it   mi cyaan
                                                 believe it
mi seh mi cyaan believe it   mi seh mi
                                                 cyaan believe it

Mi daughter bwoyfren name
is Sailor
an im pass through de port
like a ship
more gran pickney fi feed   pickney ...
but de whole a wi in need

what a night what a plight
an we cyaan get a bite   ... cyaan get a bite
me life is a stiff fight
an mi cyaan believe it   ... mi cyaan believe it
mi seh mi cyaan believe it   mi seh mi cyaan believe it

Sittin on de corner wid mi fren
talkin bout tings an time
mi hear one voice seh
'Who dat?'
[... hesitates]
[SUZANNE: 'Who dat?'
Mi seh 'A who dat?'
'A who dat a seh who dat   JOAN
when mi seh who dat?']   You've lost me

When yuh tek a stock
dem lick we dung flat
teet start fly   teet start fly
an big man start cry
an mi cyaan believe it   an mi cyaan believe it
mi seh mi cyaan believe it   ... cyaan believe it

De odder day mi pass one yard
pan de hill
When mi teck a stock
me hear 'Hey bwoy!'
'Yes, Mam?' 'Hey bwoy!'   ... bwoy
'Yes, Mam?' 'Yuh clean up
de dawg shit?'   [laughter]
'Yes, Mam'
An mi cyaan believe it
mi seh mi cyaan believe it

Doris a modder of four
get a wuk as a domestic
boss man move een
an bap [hesitates] she pregnant
again

[ADEELA: bap si kaisico]

an mi cyaan ...

[FIONA: What's bap si kaisico?]

[ADEELA: Bap, bap. She becomes pregnant.
She becomes pregnant when he baps she
kaisico]

                                                             [laughter]

[CLAUDIA: Get baps, bwoy! Baps.]   [laughs]

Dah yard de odder night
when mi hear 'Fire'
'Fire, to plate [hesitates] claat!'
Who dead? You dead?
Who dead? Me dead?
Who dead? Harry dead?

Who dead? Eleven dead
Wooeeeeeeee   [laughter]
Orange Street fire deh pan me head
an mi cyaan believe it
mi seh mi cyaan believe it

Lawd, mi see some black bud   ... black bud
livin inna one buildin
but no rent no pay
so dem cyaan stay
Lawd [hesitates ... Suz ...]

[SUZANNE: Lawd, de oppress an de
dispossess
cyaan get no res
What nex?]

reads to the end of the poem:

Teck a trip from Kingston
to Jamaica
Teck twelve from a dozen
an mi see mi Muma in heaven
MAD OUSE! MAD OUSE!
mi seh mi cyaan believe it   mi seh mi
                                                     cyaan believe it
                                                     CYNTHIA
                                                     mi seh mi
mi seh mi cyaan believe it   cyaan believe it

Yuh believe it?
How yuh fi believe it
when yuh laugh
yuh blind yuh eye to it?
But me know yuh believe it   CYNTHIA
mi know yuh believe it ...   Yeah, mi know
                                                     yuh believe it man
                                                     [laughter]

BARBARA: Cynthia wants to read it.

[a question I didn't hear]

SUZANNE: Go on then, read it.
CYNTHIA: I pick up the words from her that's
why.

First, the students want to establish for themselves whether this is a language and if so, what kind of language it is. Fiona sees it as a form of English which is distorted:

FIONA: It's like ahm ... he says 'mi seh mi cyaan believe it'. Why can't he just say 'I just couldn't believe it'? [a high-pitched tone emphasising falseness and formality]
CLAUDIA: Because it's not English though, it's yardy.
FIONA: I'm not in the mood for that kind of lingo, man.

Seeing the language on the page is particularly difficult. It is surprising, because it is a form which they associate with oral rather than written language. It is very difficult to negotiate as a written form because the distinctions of tone and pronunciation become blurred. All the 'h's' are left in the spellings of words, whereas orally, and when Mikey recited, they were aspirated. The changes in the spelling to reflect the phonetic changes seem arbitrary; words like 'fire' have been left when 'fyah' might have been more accurate. It would have been very difficult, given the similarity of the written form to Standard English, for the students to recognise it as a language as opposed to a deviation. Their confusion over its identity is reflected in the discussion about the film *The Harder They Come*:

ADEELA: It's like learning another language.
FIONA: It's like ahm, that film when they showed it on telly, *The Harder They Come* and they had subtitles. I thought it was really funny. I was laughing. [laughing]
?: Why?
FIONA: I thought people could understand it.
[Everyone talks at once]
FIONA: It's the way it's written this. I'm not talking about the language. It's the way it's written. I'm talking about THIS not the language itself.
BARBARA: That's how he speaks, how he writes.
CLAUDIA: He's expressing himself like he wants to.
SUZANNE: What was that, Havnell?
[She repeats]
HAVNELL: It was so funny because they had subtitles but I thought they were supposed to be speaking in English.

SUZANNE: Do you think everyone could understand it though?

FIONA: Yeah, I could understand it.

JOAN: This is like the North. You know when they speak it's like a different language.

SUZANNE: But you can feel the gist of it.

JOAN: Yeah, But I'd imagine it's like this. When they speak it fast, then you can't understand it at all.

ADEELA: Sometimes I couldn't. [She is referring to the film]

[Everyone at once. The tape is unclear here.]

Their concern at the negative associations of Creole underlies the discussion and is expressed by Julie, who also makes the important point that the choice of Creole is a conscious and deliberate one, not one made by default. I think, however, that she wants to redeem the poets by saying they can speak 'properly' if they want to:

> JULIE: But Suzanne, most of them, it's not all the writers who speak like that, even though they write poems like that. If you take Louise Bennett for instance, she writes a lot of patois poems but she speaks proper English.

Claudia's experience of school is another example of their recognition of Creole's negative value, particularly in the school's culture:

> CLAUDIA: When I was at school, I used to feel bad, you know. I wrote how I spoke and they made me go into tutorial classes.

She feels that her language led to her rejection in schools and as a result her whole experience before coming to England was of being devalued and dismissed. She makes the association between herself and the poet and thinks that his language represents his 'real' self in the same way that her language identified her. She recognises that he has to assert that right because, as in her experience, language carries with it social and political significance. Her account is of both the 'difference' in language varieties and of the values attached to the difference:

TINA: He should just make it easy and say what he means: '... boss man move een ... I-N in I-N.'

Tina, however, feels that to identify with the language as a language would be to identify with its implications of inferiority.

What is clear from the classroom discourse is that the poem's language represents a whole culture and experience which they don't expect to see represented in the classroom. The language draws attention to the fact that it is a human creation; that it is created in struggle and conflict. The production and reproduction of meaning is a continuous human activity, by turns reflecting the language's history of dominance and resistance and the contradictory meanings in its present-day use. A poem such as this provides an excellent way into a discussion of the nature of language and the context of its production.

It was clear, however, as I read and reread the transcript, that the context which would have made the poem's meaning for the students was missing from the lesson. Their questions resonate unanswered in the text. I have included the lesson, however, because I consider that it provides compelling evidence against the version of multi culturalism outlined in the first chapter, which argues that students need to be familiar with Black literature and culture because it represents their experiences and provides an immediate form of identification. The relationship of the majority of people – working-class, non-white, women – to a language is a complex one. If the inclusion of Creole in a curriculum in which mostly Black students participate is made arbitrarily, without the kind of context which makes its linguistic significance clear, then the result may be that students are confused, which in turn leads to or confirms their rejection of the language.

Languages of Opposition

In her book *The Education of the Black Child in Britain* Maureen Stone writes:

> it is the job of the school to enable children to function with ease in the standard language. By the same token it is the job of the home, family and community to keep the dialect alive. (1981, p. 111)

While I agree with her description, in the chapter 'Multiracial Education', of the failure of multiracial initiatives in language, I would disagree with her analysis of the reason for its failure. To argue that the 'home, family and community' should and could keep the 'dialect alive' is to gloss over the often ambivalent relationship which Caribbean people have to Creole. Many of the negative values associated with the language historically have been absorbed and are perpetuated in Black families and communities. This is reflected in the students' own attitude to it. Fiona's comments do not suggest that she is clear about the language's function as a source of, as Stone would describe it, 'self esteem and the basis of an alternative value system since the times of slavery' (ibid., p.115).

Success in the education system is still very much dependent on a kind of total immersion in the dominant culture. This means that Black students who succeed educationally lose, to some extent, their facility with their first language, usually Creole. The division which the language signifies does to some extent still exist. Julie's ambivalence and Tina's resistance illustrate the fact that they associate Creole with failure, particularly in terms of school and the classroom.

This is compounded in part by the practical implementation of a multicultural approach to language, which has resulted in Black students, who have been judged failures, being given dialect poetry as part of a 'cooling out' strategy. It is important to recognize, however, that the answer is not that schools should ignore the students' language and culture. On the contrary, they should be used as the basis for an approach to language and literature teaching which enables students to understand both the process of language-making and the historical, political and social contexts in which it is produced. An examination of the relationship between Standard English and Creole provides the basis for an analysis of all languages, not as objective forms but as 'coextensive' – to use Raymond Williams's term – with all forms of human and social activity. The lesson shows that students need to be made explicitly aware of the relationship between language, individual speakers and society, in order to make meaning from the poem. An awareness of this kind cannot, however, be restricted to an examination of Creole or of work in a dialect, but should be an integral part of all language teaching. So an understanding of the historical and social circumstances which led to the emergence of Standard English is equally important. In this way, students understand why certain language forms rather than others confer status and power in specific circumstances.

The theoretical outline which follows directed me to an understanding of the kind of ideological context which I, as a teacher, needed to be aware of in order properly to answer the students' questions.

Raymond Williams's study of linguistic method in *Marxism and Literature* is a useful starting point, because of the historical context in which he places his analysis. He makes the important connection between linguistic study and contemporary philosophies and looks at the relationship between the shifts in emphasis in linguistics and the changes in political and cultural ideologies. He begins by tracing the foundation of idealist thought to the Platonic ideal of 'name', representing something essential in nature. Later, however, language and reality were seen as separate, thus leading to the investigation of language as written texts which were seen as representations of material reality. This was particularly evident in medieval studies of grammar which, Williams argues, analysed 'the activity of language' rather than 'language as an activity'.

Eighteenth-century philosophers and historians Vico, Herder and later Humboldt centred their studies of language on the theoretical premiss that verbal language was a distinctively human 'opening of and opening to the world'. This analysis became lost, however, in the growing tendency to emphasize art and science as distinct classifications. Humboldt's theory was associated with the artistic, idealist tradition. The progress made into an investigation of language as a human activity and as 'constitutively human' was temporarily lost, with the growth of the scientific and objective approach which has characterised modern linguistics.

Williams criticises scientific theories of language – structuralisms of the kind outlined by Saussure, culminating in the works of Chomsky – because they lack a material and historical base:

> [History] in its most specific, active and connecting senses has disappeared (in one tendency has been theoretically excluded) from this account of so central an activity as language.   (Williams, Raymond, 1977, p.28)

He argues that a scientific analysis of language reduces the language to a text, a fixed objective, a 'given system which has theoretical and practical priority over utterance', which he significantly describes as 'living speech'. Evidence for the studies by structuralist linguistics has tended to be taken from examples of alien and subordinate people. While these provided rich and important descriptions of language structures, they gave no indication that language was a human and social activity:

> The 'dialects' of outlying or socially inferior groups, theoretically matched against the observer's 'standard', were regarded as at most 'behaviour', rather than independent, creative, self-directing life. (ibid., p.27)

Williams uses Volosinov and Vygotsky to underpin his analysis of language as social practice. Volosinov argues that language is a human activity within a social system. Formal signs are 'internalised', and individuals use signs at their own initiative within the context of social activity. He unites concepts of 'social' and 'individual' by describing social processes as acts of individuals. An individual consciousness is thus brought about through actual social relations. Language, in this sense, is both individual production and a reflection of the laws and logic of its material production.

Volosinov would agree with Saussure that meaning is conventional, but would disagree that it is either fixed or arbitrary:

> On the contrary the fusion of formal element and meaning ... is the result of a real process of social development in the actual activities of speech and in the continuing development of language. Indeed, signs can only exist when this actual social relationship is posited. (ibid., p.37)

Importantly, he goes on to say that in practice the sign has a variable range of meanings, corresponding to the endless variety of situations within which it is actively used. It is multi-accentual, so that there exists no system of correct meanings against which shifts in performance can be measured and judged.

In *Thought and Language*, Vygotsky's analysis of the development of language in children, the author stresses the function of language as communication and the way in which historical and cultural processes determine its psychological nature and development. He also makes a parallel as well as a connection between the development of language in children and the formation of language in society. The historical changes in the structure of language are reflected in the meaning of words, which carry the implications of those changes in their many inferences and associations:

> Linguistics did not realize that in the historical evolution of language the very structure of meaning and its psychological nature also change. From primitive generalizations, verbal thought rises to the most abstract concepts. It is not merely the content of a word that changes but the way in which reality is generalised and reflected in a word. (Vygotsky, Lev, 1962, p.121)

This relationship is constructed as a consequence of Vygotsky's definition of word meaning as 'a unit of both generalized thought and social interchange'. 'Generalisation' is interchangeable here with meaning. It is the reference, for the purposes of communication, to a group or class of objects rather than to a specific object in a specific context. Conflict in the word is, therefore, inevitable. Vygotsky gives the example of a child communicating with an adult. Although they use common words, Vygotsky argues, they do not share meaning. At an early age a child invests specific objects with meaning, and the name is an inherent part of an object; whereas an adult generalises meaning. The conflict in meaning is, one would suppose, suppressed, so that although words are exchanged, full communication does not take place.

For example, a young child may use the word 'mama' to identify all members of her family. They are so defined because they share the close relationship with her which she has with her own mother; they provide in similar ways and display the same kind of affection towards her. The context may make the meaning clear. In some situations it will be apparent that the child is calling the sister rather than the mother, whereas in others there can be conflict between the meaning intended by the child and the interpretation given to the word by the hearer.

Conflict in meaning also occurs in linguistic exchanges between adults because of the changed and changing meanings in the 'historical evolution of language'. Languages have developed historically, in the same way that concept formation develops in children and adolescents: from the concrete or syncretic, to the abstract. Meanings in present-day languages have evolved in the later stages of this process and reflect not conceptual but complex thought in Vygotsky's terms: categorisation according to experience rather than abstraction. Thus the connection between the various meanings of words seems arbitrary, though they are in fact related in the same way that connections are made in complex or everyday thought. Vygotsky gives examples of the evolutionary history of words to illustrate this and suggests that words continue to be used in a way which does not express their essential – abstract – meaning:

> the result is a ceaseless struggle within the developing language between conceptual thought and the heritage of thinking in complexes.
>
> (ibid., p. 74)

While more recent sociolinguistic studies by Trudgill (1985) and Labov (1976) and the work of ethnographers such as Dell Hymes (1971) and Shirley Brice-Heath (1983) have gone a long way towards providing social and communicative contexts for their investigation of language, a material and historical base for their study is not clearly defined. In these studies the significance of the social relations in which languages are made and change is seen as secondary and is inferred rather than placed centrally. While they are extremely important, and should not be abandoned as studies of difference, the difference they describe is not explored. What they want to assert is the equal richness and complexity of each language variety, so that languages are not labelled as inferior versions of a standard. They do not, therefore, examine the political fact that the historical contexts in which languages are produced mean that for the user their value is relative. They leave out all sense of conflict.

Raymond Williams's account of 'The Growth of Standard English' in *The Long Revolution* focuses on the struggle for

meaning in language. As a historical analysis his account has at
its centre an analysis of the social and political relations within
which languages are created. 'Standard English' in its spoken
form was, he says, the creation of a rising middle class who
wished to preserve a common, class-distinctive speech which
extended across regional barriers. Thus there developed an
'artificially' created language, with 'correct' forms of pronunciation and spelling, and so on, and the establishment of a
superior dialect by a more powerful class. Williams argues,
however, that the pre-eminence of 'Standard English' has not
been maintained. Languages change with changes in social
formation. Urbanisation has meant that the distinctions between
dialects are being minimised, and the political and cultural
dominance of America has had the effect of modifying the
sounds which are identified as 'Received Standard'.

The development of Creole serves as another example of the
importance of power relations to the growth of language systems.
It shows that the fusion of formal element and meaning exists
in social relations. Kamau Brathwaite, in *The History of the
Voice*, describes Creole as a 'strategy':

> the slave is forced to use a certain kind of language in order to disguise
> himself, to disguise his personality and to retain his culture.
>
> (Brathwaite, Kamau, 1984, p.16)

Creole is, therefore, a conscious act of human preservation
and cultural creation within the context of oppression. Creole
languages were created as the result of the economic pressures
for communication between different ethnic groups. Pidgin –
the basis out of which Creole languages grew – developed as a
result of the need for Europeans to trade with West Africa. The
Europeans did not assimilate the West African coastal languages,
but the coastal peoples were forced to adapt their language
to the Europeans. The resulting 'pidgins' maintained African
grammatical structures but emerged with European lexical
items, usually associated with business and trade. The same

process, under much harsher conditions, occurred in the Caribbean and the Americas, where the mother tongues of slaves were
suppressed through a system of dividing speakers of the same
language in order to make slave revolts more difficult. Despite
this, the Africans preserved their syntax and used the vocabu-
lary of European languages. The historical context of its creation still affects present-day attitudes to Creole and to Creole
speakers; and on the whole low status is conferred on the
language and its users. Writing over thirty years ago, and
describing French cultural imperialism in the Caribbean, which
was much more systematic and institutionalised than its British
counterpart, Frantz Fanon, in his *Black Skins White Masks,*
nevertheless provides a striking metaphor for the power and
status language acquires in societies which have been politically
dominated by Europe. He shows that language does not simply
reflect social formation but plays an active role in it. It is used
as an instrument of cultural hegemony:

> The Negro of the Antilles will be proportionately whiter – that is he will
> come closer to being a real human being in direct relation to his mastery
> of the French language.
>
> (Fanon, Frantz, 1952, p.18)

The language the 'Negro' speaks represents to the European
both an infantile expression – a non-language – and a symbol
of barbarism. Thus the white person addressing Fanon's 'Negro'
speaks using childlike expressions and adopts an attitude that
mirrors the nature of the relationship between the two language
speakers. He talks down to the Black man, 'imprisoning him,
primitivizing him, decivilizing him'. The weight of colonial
history is encapsulated in this linguistic interchange.

Fanon points out that the 'Negroes'' search for this
expression is a political act, which is continually being contested
and undermined because of its self-consciousness. While it is
attacked for being contrived, this is without regard for the fact
that as Williams has illustrated, a language like Standard English
is a conscious creation and, as Trudgill indicates, many national

languages have been selected and developed deliberately to include modern technical concepts.

The struggle within languages, which Vygotsky describes, is represented by the tension within specific words. This may be illustrated in the use of words like 'Creole' or 'pidgin'. Many speakers are reluctant to accept 'pidgin' as a valid linguistic term because of its continued use to mean 'bad' or 'broken' English and its connotations of inferiority. Similarly, for many students 'Creole' is an unfamiliar way of describing 'patois', and for most Black students born here it is an unfamiliar word.

The use of the word 'Creole' differs from culture to culture. It has both specific and unspecific meanings. The dictionary gives a precise meaning and a 'loose' meaning; 'loosely', Creole is used to describe people born in the European colonies who were of mixed parentage. It has come to mean any cultural product – food, dress – of an 'exotic' appearance or flavour. These kinds of stereotypic connotations had resulted in its less frequent use. Brathwaite (1974) traces the word's origins to two Spanish words: 'criar' – to create, to imagine, to establish, found, settle – and 'colon': a native to the settlement who is not ancestrally indigenous to it. With reference to Jamaica, he uses Creole to mean the adaptation, of all groups who are native to or born in a slave society or colony, to the culture of the environment and to the culture of other groups. The process itself involves struggle and conflict; the European culture, with its attendant messages of superiority, was forced on to the African slave. Europeans themselves had to adapt to a new social and physical environment and make appropriate tranformations of their own culture in order to survive.

Although in certain societies the term 'Creole' has retained a specific meaning to describe particular communities or cultures within that society, it is used differently in almost every case. In Brazil, for example, it was used to describe African slaves born in Brazil, whereas in Louisiana it is used to describe the French-speaking population and in New Orleans it is applied to people of mixed African and European descent. Linguistically it is used to describe language created out of a mixture of European and African influences and has only recently become popularly accepted, though still not uncontested, as a term to describe those languages. The popular stereotypes are still present for the speakers in the word itself.

It is important to note, as Williams's example of Standard English illustrates, that the relationship between societies, individuals and language is a changing and sometimes contradictory one. While on the one hand there is a low-status or negative social and political value attached to Creole, it continues to be developed, revalued and celebrated by writers and speakers who deliberately foster its use, both as a subversive means of communication and as an open, legitimate expression of cultural unity. The metaphoric structures, for example, which characterise West African languages and were used as coded or indirect means of expression during slavery have been retained in Creole structures. These elaborate structures still exist, and are being drawn attention to and 'kept alive' by poets like Louise Bennett. Students too, in some informal networks, might consciously participate in this process, although their participation is often not conscious and is effected almost by default. Students should be made conscious of the symbolic importance of Creole as a language of opposition, so that they are aware of the relationship between their use of Creole to form bonds of cultural identity and its historic functions of resistance and subversion. They should be encouraged to be aware of the political and social contexts which create these kinds of linguistic processes and their feelings of confusion or embarrassment in relation to the use of language in the classroom. Such understandings can be used to illustrate the complex and contradictory relationship of individuals to language at the level of class, race and gender.

Tony Davies (1980) gives an example of the complex relationship most comprehensive school students have to the language of schools. He argues that the concept of a 'national language' is misleading, since it is a language which most English people do not speak. It is the language reflected in what is called the body of 'national literature' and enforced through 'the coercive and compulsory routines of elementary schooling'.

Most working-class schoolchildren read and experience a language which is nominally theirs and in which they are supposed to participate and create, yet from which they feel alienated:

> Many working-class children never experience their 'own' language as anything other than an oppressive orthodoxy imposed from outside. A large number, indeed, by strategies of 'failure' and refusal manage largely to avoid even that.   (Davies, Tony, 1980, p.11)

Those who are 'won over' by the education system learn to express themselves in 'literary' language: a language which testifies to cultural superiority. There is constant conflict in language users, however, because at the same time language excludes many if not most speakers, including those who have been 'won over' and who find themselves traduced by the 'national language'. This results in a continuous struggle consciously to find ways of redefining themselves inside the language or, in the case of Standard English, on one of its 'continuums', or in languages like Creole or Black English. When Claudia says that Mikey Smith is choosing a language which represents his 'real self' she suggests that the poet feels that both he and his experience of reality have been excluded from meaningful expression in Standard English.

In *Civil Wars* June Jordan writes of the conscious celebration of language as a political symbol:

> As a Black poet and writer I am proud of our Black verbally bonding system borne of our struggle to avoid annihilation.
>
> (Jordan, June, 1981, p.69)

Her exclusion from the national language has forced her to examine the social factors which invest language with value, and she describes the contradictions for her, within a language where she finds both creative expression and critical and cultural oppression:

> As a human being, I delight in this miraculous, universal means of communication.... And I celebrate this fact of language that man and womankind have been privileged to explore and extend.... But as a Black poet and writer, I hate words that cancel my name and my history and the freedom of my future.   (ibid., p.69)

In *The African Experience in Literature and Ideology*, Abiola Irele observes that the contest and conflict is both in individual use and in its cultural and political context. His work serves as a striking example of the way in which the historical evolution of a language reflects on its present-day meanings, which are fraught with tension. He points to the fact that although African writers are often actively engaged in the fight for self-government and their work is often concerned with a criticism and rejection of European cultural values, the language they use to express that rejection and to assert national selfhood is European:

> In this one area of our deeper life, we feel in its most intense manifestation the alienation and cultural ambiguity of our colonial past.
>
> (Irele, Abiola, 1981, p.45)

This is in many cases the official language of government and higher education, yet it is often unfamiliar to the majority of the people. As a result, the work of these writers is often inaccessible to a national audience.

African writers like Ngugi Wa Thiongo and David Diop urge a resolution to the contradiction expressed by Irele and they argue that African writers should write in African languages, not in English; that they should cease to perpetuate colonial and imperialist relationships whereby the colonised enrich the culture and society of the coloniser at the expense of their own. Ngugi states that writers contribute to the growth and development of the language in which they write. In the case of African writers this should be their mother tongues, not a European language which they have to mould and shape and purge free of cultural bias before it can be used to express their own culture and environment.

In *Decolonising the Mind* (1981) Ngugi describes the experience of being schooled in Kenya, where, until 1952 when a state of emergency was declared by the colonial regime, he was educated in Gikuyu. Thereafter English became the official language of instruction:

> In Kenya, English became more than a language: it was *the* language, and all others had to bow before it in deference.

He goes on to describe the kind of humiliation pupils received if they were caught speaking Gikuyu in the area around the school:

> The culprit was given corporal punishment – three to five strokes of the cane on bare buttocks – or was made to carry a metal plate around the neck with inscriptions such as 'I AM STUPID' or 'I AM A DONKEY'.

(p.11)

He sees his task, and the task of all African writers, as one of restoring the Kenyan or African child to her own environment and constructively adding to the culture of the society. He stresses that writers have a choice of languages and that the language they choose represents the position they have adopted in relation to their environment. In writing in or continuing to write in European languages, they are firmly identifying with an elite group within their own culture and the culture of the metropolis. They are contributing to a body of literary production which excludes the development of the majority of people and by so doing entrenches the divide between themselves and the peasants or urban working classes. Those who are unschooled and are keeping the language alive, but with skills of expression only in their mother tongue, know that they will not have access to power within that society and that their contribution will go unrecognised.

Ngugi has returned to writing in Gikuyu after seventeen years of writing in English, in a conscious attempt to 'transcend colonial alienation'. However, the work of African writers to which most readers in the West have access is that which is written in a European language. There is a tendency, it would seem, to assume that if a work needs to be translated from an African language to English, for example, then the content will be inaccessible to a European audience. There are political, economic and cultural pressures on all Black writers to write in a European language and in some cases, governments are openly hostile to writers who use their mother tongue. There is mounting pressure too from within those societies for writers to take responsibility for enriching the cultural expression of their communities. These pressures and tensions are evident in much of this writing and provide evidence of the way in which the constant struggles and conflicts of the context of language-making is reflected in its use and meaning.

I would argue that as a strategy for teaching language and literature, the use of Black linguistic expression provides a clear and often literal example of the nature of language. It does so by identifying the historical and cultural struggle for meaning within language, and by demonstrating how language becomes a reflection of the political and social context of its creation. It also provides students with examples of the contradictory relation between individuals and language: one in which they sometimes uncomfortably find themselves. A close examination of 'Mi Cyaan Believe It' would provide a perfect illustration of the struggles of class and power which are the historical context of all languages. Students could then better place both their responses to the poem and the poem itself within a context which would illuminate their understanding not just of Creole but of language, its making and function.

I have felt it important to give weight to a theoretical analysis because, while the teaching of Black literature is a part of many teachers' practice, what is often missing is an ideological framework for making that linguistic literary choice. As a result, students are often left confused by the occasional appearance of

Black language forms in the classroom. I have hoped here to give some background to the questions which arise from this confusion and to indicate the kind of context needed to provide answers to such questions.

5

Classroom Discourse

The group consists of about fifteen students, ten to twelve of whom come regularly. They are in the first year of a two-year City and Guilds course which prepares them for work in nursing homes, homes for the mentally handicapped and nurseries, as unqualified assistants. All except two of the students are Black women aged between nineteen and the late forties. There was one man in the group, who was in his forties and who had a great deal of difficulty working in a class dominated by younger Black women. He has now left, but during this session he was sitting in the corner as he always did during lessons, usually reading old sociology or psychology books and taking copious notes.

The group whose discussion I taped consisted of five young women, all of about the same age. I think that Claudia and Theresa are the eldest, although they are only about twenty-two. Claudia is from Dominica and has two children. Theresa is a Grenadian, and Julie, who is about nineteen, came to England from Jamaica two years ago. I first met her at the Supplementary School where I taught when she had just arrived in England. Delores is twenty. She was born here and her parents are Jamaican. Patricia is Burmese and seems always to have identified with Caribbean culture, while at the same time retaining her identity as an Asian woman.

The abilities of the group vary widely. None of them is a

confident writer, though one or two write well. Claudia dislikes
writing and has problems with both reading and writing.

I try to use diverse material in the class as much as possible
to achieve the objectives of a Communication syllabus. This is
partly because many of the students have come from other
courses in areas like Business Studies where they followed a
similar Communication syllabus to the one designed for this
course. Most of them have had little experience of Black writing
either at school or on previous courses. I wanted to introduce
them to material which reflected Black culture and experiences,
because I feel it is important that students know that it exists.
I also thought that they might be able to relate quite easily to
the pieces I had chosen and thus be willing to participate in
discussion centred around the material; this would then provide
a useful basis for their own writing and encourage students such
as Claudia, who are reluctant to commit anything to paper,
actually to write.

During one lesson we sat round a large map of the world
and traced the spread of European languages throughout the
colonised world, looking at language divisions in the Caribbean.
I asked the students to locate where they or their parents came
from and its geographical position in relation to Britain. This
exercise alone prompted a lengthy discussion about languages
in the Caribbean and an exchange of information about the
cultures of different islands.

Fiona was amazed to discover that Guyana, where her parents
are from, was part of South America. We then had to examine
why Guyana is thought of as a West Indian island, so we began
a discussion about slavery and the history of colonialism. Some
students who were born here had been back to the West Indies
and had found it a difficult place to call 'home'. I remember
Barbara complaining about the mosquitoes and the poverty.
Fiona said that she had heard about the lack of proper toilets
and did not want to experience it.

Using the map, we traced the spread of European languages,

and the discussion was steered back to language, so we listened to Louise Bennett recite and talk about her poems. There was much more to examine, but the events surrounding the students' confrontation at the playgroup intruded into the discussion, reminding us that we are at present negotiating the legacy of the history we were discussing. It is interesting, in fact, to look back at the whole pattern of events during the year and see how inseparable attention to Black writing in the classroom is from students' own reality. To ask them to read it as discrete texts would be to undermine both the work and their experience.

I
Calypso

1

The stone had skidded arc'd and bloomed into islands:
Cuba and San Domingo
Jamaica and Puerto Rico
Grenada Guadeloupe Bonaire

curved stone hissed into reef
wave teeth fanged into clay
white splash flashed into spray
Bathsheba Montego bay

bloom of the arcing summers . . .

2

The islands roared into green plantations
ruled by silver sugar cane
sweat and profit
cutlass profit
islands ruled by sugar cane

And of course it was a wonderful time
a profitable hospitable well-worth-your-time

when captains carried receipts for rices
letters spices wigs
opera glasses swaggering asses
debtors vices pigs

O it was a wonderful time
an elegant benevolent redolent time –
and young Mrs P.'s quick irrelevant crime
at four o'clock in the morning ...

3

But what of black Sam
with the big splayed toes
and the shoe black shiny skin?

He carries bucketfulls of water
'cause his Ma's just had another daughter.

And what of John with the European name
who went to school and dreamt of fame
his boss one day called him a fool
and the boss hadn't even been to school ...

4

Steel drum steel drum
hit the hot calypso dancing
hot rum hot rum
who goin' stop this bacchanalling?

For we glance the banjo
dance the limbo
grow our crops by maljo

have loose morals
gather corals
father our neighbour's quarrels

perhaps when they come
with their cameras and straw
hats: sacred pink tourists from the frozen Nawth

we should get down to those

white beaches
where if we don't wear breeches

it becomes an island dance
Some people doin' well
while others are catchin' hell

o the boss gave our Johnny the sack
though we beg him please
please to take 'im back

so the boy now nigratin' overseas ...

Shortly after the series of lessons I have described, I asked
them to look at 'Calypso', a poem I like very much and
which I thought would be accessible to them. They worked in
groups because they seem to enjoy that mode of working.
It is a way of involving everyone in classroom discussion,
as everyone has a chance to talk and to listen to each other's
contribution, without feeling that someone is censoring their
interpretation.

SUZANNE: Do you know what calypso is? What's a calypso?
FIONA: Don't really know how to describe it. Ahm ...
BARBARA: Calypso? Calypso music. I don't know how to say it.
JULIE: Calypso, calypso [singing]. Can't describe it really.
[Laughter]
SUZANNE: Can you try and put it into words?
PAT: It's a fast beat isn't it?
JULIE: You know [moving around]. Yeah. It's energetic isn't it?
DELORES: It's dancing as well isn't it?

We read the poem a few times. I asked the question 'what's a
calypso?' because I thought that a discussion about calypso
music would provide a context within which they could discuss
the way the poem related to the calypso form, with its ironies
and innuendos. The above transcript is all I could decipher
from the tape on which there was at least five minutes of
the whole class talking, laughing and singing. The lesson was
interrupted and when we resumed I stopped participating,
leaving them with a few general questions about the poem.

The group I taped enjoyed their interaction with the poem immensely. There was laughter and enthusiasm for the discussion. They created a calypso of their own, illuminating the poet's descriptions and insights with their own experiences. Their discourse bears all the features of that artistic form: humour, play on words, discussion about mundane occurrences in the Caribbean. The framework for this creation of theirs is their reference to the romantic ideal of the Caribbean which punctuates their discussion and might be compared to the 'bacchanalling' rhythm of calypso music, which provides a frame or even a disguise for serious descriptions of suffering, oppression and corruption, as well as a means of relating anecdotes about everyday events:

CLAUDIA: At home they sing for everything. My granny is singing and chopping wood.

PAT: Chopping wood?

CLAUDIA: Yeah. Chopping wood and moving.

JULIE: Oh, oh, oh, oh. [singing and shaking her body]

PAT: Yeah. I've seen them dance. They lift up their skirts and that. And the expression on their faces! Lifting up their skirts though. Right up!

CLAUDIA: That's the custom though, innit?

PAT: I wouldn't dance it.

CLAUDIA: If you could dance [laughing], you would dance it.

DELORES: Yeah, at this party, right, this woman was all over the place. One minute she was here at one end of the room and then she would be gone again. You should've seen her.

CLAUDIA: Yeah I know.

PAT: Slackness [laughing]. What're we gonna put then? Where are you from then?

CLAUDIA: Dominica.

THERESA: I grew up with calypso.

CLAUDIA: There's a song for everything. If you go toilet they sing it, if you pick figs they sing it.

THERESA: You know, there was a song about Princess Anne when she visit Grenada an' like there'd be a song about Charles and Diana, anything that happens; 'Sparrow, Sparrow's' the best though. [A tapping noise]

JULIE: Now.

PAT: You've just come, Julie, you should know all about it.

JULIE: I don't really know nothing about it. In Jamaica you know like, they don't really play it as such. Not the young people.

The students identify the calypso as a form of commentary on both the trivial and the important. The calypsonian has traditionally come from and represented the views of the majority. On one level his survival was based on the offerings of the poor, a drink in a bar, a meal, payment for him to make up a tune about anything which caught their fancy, either in the immediate environment or in the community. He would also take on the role of their defender against the injustices of the ruling elite; he could not be effectively silenced by them, because he was their entertainer, and despite his thinly veiled attacks on them there would always be, in the same song, other themes; humour, bawd; bits of 'ole gossip' to which they could jump and fête.

Though less comprehensive, the students' description is not far removed from the following explanation of the role and function of the calypsonian in Trinidadian society. In *The Trinidad Calypso* Warner describes an incident where Stalin, a popular calypsonian, caused great controversy about his title-winning song, which dealt with the sensitive issue of race in Trinidad society. The song highlighted the antagonism amongst different racial and cultural groups. He writes:

> Stalin's views were debated with all the seriousness befitting an academic paper. Stalin was interviewed on radio and television and was asked questions that should really have been put to the Caricom Secretary General. His views were taken as the collective voice of Caribbean Blacks.
>
> (Warner, 1982, p. 85)

He continues with the general observation that

> [the calypsonian] interprets that which is new and foreign, as can be seen from the many calypsos commenting on world affairs, from King Edward's abdication to Princess Margaret's wedding; from Mussolini's invasion of Ethiopia to the downfall of Adi Amin and Bokassa.   (ibid., p. 87)

The students took a long time actually to commit a definition of 'calypso' to writing. They eventually wrote:

> The rhythm of the calypso once you've heard it just wants you to let loose
> and it creates an atmosphere of happiness and excitement all around you.

Peter and the group he worked with produced a more formal and technical description:

> It is a rhythm produced by the native population of the Caribbean and
> Central America. It includes bongo drums and other percussion instru-
> ments whose origins are in Africa.

This response illustrates the student's distance, which he emphasises by physically distancing himself during the discussion from this cultural form.

The former group's writing and discussion showed how the poem enabled them to bring something of themselves, their culture and experience, to the classroom. That interaction gave them the confidence to talk with authority about their own experience and about the meaning of the poem.

My analysis of the discussion was helped by Jane Miller's account of a living 'tradition' of literature, where readers and writers actively engage with the text to produce meaning. Fundamental to that redefinition of tradition is the concept of language as an active, human creation and of meaning as being created in social intercourse. The discourses of students' personal history, the history of imperialism and their classroom interaction, create the circumstances for this particular interpretation of the text:

> Children make stories and poems and pictures and the world they live in
> *mean* something, and they make that meaning through negotiating between
> what they already know, what they are coming to know and what writers
> and story-tellers have made for them. The *making* is active and must
> continue to be.   (Miller, Jane, 1984, p. 8)

Two particular characteristics of calypso are taken up: one by Patricia, who comments on the abandon which the music inspires:

> Steel drum steel drum
> hit the hot calypso dancing

Her use of 'I've seen them' places her at some distance from the 'calypso culture', and she continues 'they lift up their skirts and that'. Delores too comments on the spectacle created by the dancing and, in her case, the dancers' total surrender to the music. Claudia and Theresa, however, remind the students of the role of calypso in people's everyday lives: it is a release from the drudgery and the hard labour in the fields and on small farms. Delores learns from Claudia's and Theresa's discussion. She echoes the connection with her remark: 'singing while they're cutting'. Claudia notes, to Pat's surprise, that there is no distinction in the rural Caribbean between men's and women's work; women and children chop wood.

They identify calypso as a form of reporting and news-carrying in a society still strongly influenced and shaped by oral cultural expression. The last remark on the transcript takes the form of the calypso idiom, – a glancing comment, with a play on words about a small, perhaps insignificant incident the singer observes.

I took a cough sweet from a student, but had to spit it out because it was so hot:

CLAUDIA: Feeling hot, hot, hot. [Words of a popular calypso song. She sings]

Claudia's exuberance has helped to inspire the rest of the group. She has come into her own during this discussion. The fact that she relates so closely to the images in the poem has given her a rare opportunity to speak authoritatively. Others were able to learn from her and had to listen to her; this marked an important shift in her relationship with the group. Usually she sits with Delores and has to defer to her, since Delores is a more fluent and confident writer:

CLAUDIA: I said 'fiery colour'. You should write down what I say. No big words. You try too hard. And you gone to the dictionary. Don't bother with the dictionary.

I have noticed that although Theresa is a much quieter person she responds very intensely to lessons which involve reading about a Black experience. Significantly, she chose to write her own ideas, whereas the others were glad of an opportunity not to have to write anything. As part of an explanation of what a calypso is, she wrote one of her own.

Together, the group share experiences in order to describe the role of calypso in Caribbean society; they are also able to identify the ironic relationship between its form, its content and its function in society. Meaning is shaped in the classroom in the interaction between the poem, the various experiences which the students bring to the text and the particular context of a group discussion.

Claudia's response to Patricia – 'if you could dance you would dance it' – suggests that the poem has prompted them to place themselves in relation to it and to each other; to identify themselves and their origins and to try to connect their histories. Pat's response throughout is to 'place' everyone, to locate the text in relation to her experience of the other women in the group. Each responds, showing diverse experiences. Having observed that the meanings the students are making begin with their own experiences, she is waiting for Julie's contribution. Julie makes the important point that 'calypso' is not a form which dominates all Caribbean experiences:

JULIE: It's a fertile land, isn't it?

CLAUDIA: The country part is green and sweet-smelling. When you're running in the field you get cut up and you have to run quick to get the firewood.

THERESA: I never had to chop any.

CLAUDIA: You're lucky, you get spoil. I'd love to go back. My mum's going back next year. You know we used to throw stones and pretend it was money. All those stupid things. There was red sand as well. I used to say 'look gran, we're rich' and she just box me – don't be so stupid.

THERESA: They weren't stupid. It was fun.

PAT: You sound like John. He's always saying 'when I was little in Barbados . . .'.

THERESA: When I got here all I can remember is crying, crying.

CLAUDIA: Yeah, my mum – because I never used to call my mum 'mum'. Mum was granny, you know.

SUZANNE: How old were you when you came here?

CLAUDIA: Eight, and then I came back again when I was thirteen. I couldn't stand it yunno. I wish I'd never left there.

THERESA: And it was raining and cold. We came in November and my mum said if I stopped crying she'd send me home.

CLAUDIA: And you still here [laughing]. I said to my mother she should never have left, you know – isn't it Suzanne? All this backwards and forwards.

SUZANNE: Yes. I was with my grandparents as well. Our parents couldn't really have afforded to send for us at the time. Things were very hard here. Anyway ...

JULIE: You remember 'jump'?

CLAUDIA: Yeah. Jump means licks. Bring down your knickers ...

Again, Claudia's remark encapsulates the juxtaposition of romance and realism, a traditional feature of calypso. Julie later brings in the 'licks', or beatings: an essential part of a Caribbean childhood experience. The discussion inevitably moved to the subject of 'home' and leaving. It seems as if it is difficult to see images of the Caribbean without thinking of loss and separation. Theresa and Claudia associate memories of childhood with the loss of a time and place which symbolise freedom and innocence.

The ease with which they switch from the poem to their experiences shows the kind of confidence they feel with the material. This confidence is also evident in their poetic account of what they imagine or remember to be the 'bloom of the arcing summers'. Their celebration of this image is what struck me initially about their response, particularly as I listened to their discussion of the poem. I broke off my interjection with ' ... anyway' because I was anxious that they should get on with looking more closely at the text. When I examined it again more carefully I realised that they had in fact made reference to a less idealised reality.

Delores, who has never been to the Caribbean, gives a picture-postcard account of the islands and is immediately corrected by

Claudia, who talks of hurricanes and 'black' sand:

DELORES: Well, there's flowers and palm trees and golden sand.
CLAUDIA: Black. Sometimes the sand is black. Right now with the hurricane
  season, it's black. I wouldn't go there now. It's nice when it rains, though.
  In September, it's rainy and windy. And then it's not safe to go into the
  sea at night.
THERESA: It's the curve of the moon in the sea bed. I mean river bed.
PAT: Sea or river?
CLAUDIA: Yeah. It's fantastic when the moon shines on the river bed. It's
  a beautiful fiery colour.
DELORES: Fiery?
CLAUDIA: Am I lying? It's fantastic!
DELORES: Anyway, I'll be there one day.

They produce a poetic discourse of their own. Claudia creates
an image which seems strange to the others. She relishes her
own lyricism and is confident that her experience makes her
statement valid and accurate. Julie too joins in the production.
They use the language of the poem as a basis from which to
experiment with language form and to give new expression to
their experience:

JULIE: It's the sweet juice trickling down your throat.
CLAUDIA: Rippling.
JULIE: It makes you dribble. Sweet juicy liquid. You can write that.
CLAUDIA: Sweet juicy liquid, you can't say that.
JULIE: Of course you can.

Delores's comment about the golden sand indicates something
of the complex relationship between those first- and second-
generation young people of Caribbean descent born here; adults,
like their parents, who were born and spent their early adulthood
there; and young women like Claudia and Theresa, who spent
their childhood in the Caribbean. The longing for relief from
an embattled existence here has resulted in the constant reproduction of the romantic ideal. Although it does not represent,
for a younger generation like Delores, a concrete reality, it has
become the cornerstone of their identity. In all the talk and

reminiscing about 'home', Delores feels it important to assert:
'I'll be there one day'. When Delores talks about the golden
sand she is informed by her parents, by popular culture and,
particularly, by song lyrics. Her parents, like Johnny 'nigratin'
overseas', came to England only out of economic necessity; here,
culturally and socially, politically and economically, they are
'niggers'. She takes over the writing from Pat in order to be
able to express fully her contribution to the discussion, and she
writes:

> the weather is continuously hot and the land is filled of bright green grass,
> blooming flowers with lovely blossoms and beautiful water falls and elegant
> palm trees.

Although this is not quite the interpretation of 'bloom of the
arcing summers' that I had expected, their comments do touch
on important questions, as the answer indicates what the exile –
and the poet himself – remembers, and the group is justified
in interpreting 'bloom of arcing summers' as a celebration.
Brathwaite himself uses it in poems like 'South', where he
returns 'home' after years exiled in the 'lands of the north'.
This is the longing the students have inherited from their
parents and from their culture – a whole people's idealisation of
their inheritance.

PAT: Theresa's boyfriend's got fifteen kids.
THERESA: Of course.
PAT: Fifteen?
CLAUDIA: It's like this man, right ...
THERESA: You believe me, don't you?
CLAUDIA: Seriously though, not fifteen but thirteen. He's got at least
    thirteen. Two here, one there. He's really bad you know, children every-
    where, one here and one here.

As I have indicated, however, their perceptions of the 'ideal' do
not completely block their ability to recognise the political and
economic realities in their reading. They explain the ironies,
picking out 'loose morals', which is the colonial explanation of

what seems to be social anarchy, and comment on 'sweat and profit':

> The slaves worked hard for nothing and their white owners shipped the profit out of the country. Life on the plantation was hard.

One group (not this one), when asked what they thought of the poem, wrote that they were surprised that the Caribbean was only for tourists. They had thought that it was for Black people and others living there to enjoy.

Joan, who worked on her own, wrote this description of the plantation:

> The plantation seemed to be a happy place, although the work was hard, bodies full of sweat while cane was being cut. Strong smelling fragrance of cane blending in with slow graceful movements.

Again, the student has produced her own form of lyricism. She was the only student who gave that kind of interpretation, partly because she worked on her own and did not have the benefit of discussion in a group, and partly because, as the following extracts show, she uses her experience and her reading to resist making political meanings, particularly ones which imply, or explicitly describe, racial exploitation.

Both this account and the following one raise important questions about the process by which meaning is produced. The fact that 'Calypso' has been signalled to the class as a poem – that is, 'literature' to be 'studied' in a classroom – has alerted the students to the language and poetic form, whereas if the poem had been a song they heard at a party they would have been less likely to wrestle with the words and their meaning. During the discussion they draw, from deep within themselves, buried memories of the Caribbean, and in the process of making sense of the poem to themselves and to others in the group they reflect, draw connections with each other's histories, and come to terms with the more painful aspects of their childhood.

EXTRACTS FROM A DISCUSSION OF 'MI CYAAN BELIEVE IT'

Aspects of the following transcript are examined in detail in Chapters
1 and 2. I have included extracts of the discussion here as further
evidence of the students' active participation in the production of
meaning which characterises the discourse analysed above. These
examples show how important students' experiences are in the nego-
tiation of meaning and illustrate how their experiences interact with
the text, the classroom context and the reality outside the classroom:

SUZANNE: What other impressions do you get of the place he's talking about?
FIONA: What place is he talking about anyway? Is it Jamaica or the West
Indies or what sort of place?
TINA: Kingston. Kingston's Jamaica?
ADEELA: 'Tek a trip from Kingston' ... What does it mean here?
FIONA: Tek a trip from Kingston / to Jamaica / Tek twelve from a dozen /
What's that anyway? [giggles]
SUZANNE: It's the confusion, I think ... he's trying to say that the things
he sees are all a riddle to him. Like when he says 'MAD OUSE'.
BARBARA: Pressure tek him.
JULIE: Orange Street is Kingston.
SUZANNE: If the poem didn't say Kingston ... sorry.
JOAN: Or a place like Kingston. Somewhere in Kingston where he lives.
SUZANNE: Yeah. A particular area. And what about the people who live
there?

This is a difficult section of the poem. They try to place the
poem in the framework of references to their own experiences
and knowledge. Julie untangles some of the confusion the students have trying to 'place' the poem. In fact only Havnell, Julie
and I would know where Orange Street is or anything about
the Orange Street fire. Joan abstracts the poem from its concrete
context and then moves on to be more specific. Examples in
an earlier chapter show that she is often able to distance herself
from the actual language or images in the text in order to
understand it. In the process, she makes interesting analogies
with experiences which are more familiar to her.

Barbara's 'pressure tek him' shows that as in the last
discussion, they elaborate on the poem by using its particular

linguistic form, which results in a kind of participation:

FIONA: His daughter [reads]
Mi daughter bwoyfren name is Sailor
  an im pass through de port like a ship
  more gran pickney fi feed
  but de whole a we in need.
SUZANNE: That's a regular saying, isn't it? – he passes through like a sailor.
ADEELA: He comes through and drop one and run off.
CLAUDIA: I didn't hear that.
FIONA: The ship comes into the port.
CLAUDIA: Yeah, the sailors come into the port and then 'drop' and go off again. [laughs]

Adeela, like Barbara, embellishes the poem, using its language. Claudia and Adeela explore the image on their own and work out all its connotations. In the following extract Adeela associates the rough intimidation the poet describes – 'who dat?' – with her memory of the lawlessness of the police. Joan's reading is different, and her questioning helps to clarify meaning; the reading of the poem in these two examples gives the students scope to bring into the classroom aspects of their culture and experience which do not normally have a place there:

SUZANNE: Apart from the poverty, what else strikes you?
ADEELA: Police, police brutality.
SUZANNE: Yeah ... if you think there's police brutality here ...
BARBARA: Yeah.
SUZANNE: What are the police like?
BARBARA: Dangerous.
CLAUDIA: Deadly. They call out to you and stop you and boom!
JOAN: That missed me. I thought I was getting the gist of it, but I can't see anything about the police.
SUZANNE: No, not directly. I suppose Adeela means like, 'Who dat? / Mi seh "a who dat?" / "A who dat a seh who dat when mi seh who dat?"'
CLAUDIA: They come and surprise you with violence.
JOAN: Oh I see. I thought I'd lost you all. What do they look like?
BARBARA: Rugged.

[Now everyone at once] Like ... they have dark suits with white stripes / tight trousers and big black riding boots / they look real nice.

CLAUDIA: They question you. Yeah, you know what I mean ... then boom!
BARBARA: And they look lovely and shiny if they're dark.
ADEELA: ... didn't know they carry guns.
BARBARA: Yeah.

The following is an interesting section, showing Julie providing information from her experience to illuminate the poem, Barbara using the poem and the discussion to clarify something in her own experience, and Joan unable to accept the interpretation the others provide:

SUZANNE: De odder day me pass one yard
        pan de hill
        When mi tek a stock
        me hear 'Hey bwoy!'

JULIE: Red Hills.
SUZANNE: What is he describing there? What, whose attitude?
CLAUDIA: Rich women and servants.
JULIE: They pass the gates. If the women got work.
SUZANNE: Why does he have her call him 'bwoy'?
FIONA: White people do call Black people boy.
ADEELA: Like house boys.
CLAUDIA: 'Cause they're above them.
JOAN: Well, my dad calls me girl even now.
SUZANNE: But why is he being called 'bwoy' by her?
FIONA: He doesn't earn as much money as she does, I suppose.
CLAUDIA: Like a slave.
BARBARA: In general, though, in Jamaica people do call others like that, like my cousin, he was much younger than me and he was calling me a girl.
SUZANNE: I think that with women it's different.
ADEELA: Ah in South Africa you're a boy, never a man.
SUZANNE: And that's really important, because it's meant to deliberately take away from their manhood. When a woman's called a girl, she's flattered, isn't she?
JOAN: I'd just think he's being funny.
FIONA: Hey, young girl [in an American accent].
CLAUDIA: [Laughs] Yes.
SUZANNE: There are different connotations, aren't there? If someone called out to your boyfriend, 'hey young boy!'
BARBARA: [Laughs] Who y'a call bwoy?

Joan is annoyed that race has had explicitly to come into the discussion. She would be more comfortable with the language if it were just an abstract form, but the fact that it isn't causes problems, and she has similar problems with the images which suggest racial oppression. The students use their knowledge of who the 'oppress' and the 'dispossess' are, traditionally, to understand the poem. Immediately, Fiona relates it to Black and white relationships, though in fact the poet is probably referring more specifically to class oppression. Adeela's understanding of the class and power dynamics represented in the term 'bwoy' is clear, and at the end of this part of the discussion I think most of the students understand the significance of the image. Joan, however, persists in her own interpretation.

The reasons for her and others' resistance have been explored in earlier chapters. The social and political implications of both poems are so integral to their meaning that they cannot be ignored, and as both transcripts show, the readers' experience is an essential factor in the production and creation of meaning. Friction can be caused, as the students' understandings of the poem conflict. (The context of the texts' production is inevitably a factor in the production of meaning in the classroom.)

In the next chapter I shall look at a theoretical framework which may be able to take into account, when analysing the activity of reading, the experiences of the reader and the context of the texts' production.

6

Beyond Theories of Exclusion

The form and the content of both poems discussed in the previous chapter speak overtly of their histories and the circumstances of their production. As a result, these texts sit uneasily in the classroom; students are forced to recognise both the context of the poems' production and the present context of their reading. Both considerations further challenge ideas about literature and the social and cultural construction of a reader of literature. Before examining the nature of that challenge, it is important to show the ways in which literary theories which have dominated literature teaching have excluded Black writing.

Leavis has become important to the teaching of literature because he hardened the criteria by which texts might be selected for study; those texts would be the substance of the 'great tradition' of English writing. Literature thus becomes a commodity which can be packaged to rest neatly in the curriculum, to be taught and assessed. The value of Leavis to contemporary traditions of criticism and to educationalists is that in this opposition to the 'middlebrow' culture of the nineteenth- and early-twentieth-century salon society, he gave to criticism an intellectual rigour it had previously lacked.

Leavis's focus was the text, which should, he claimed, reflect its own values and experiences. He stressed the need for the 'scrutiny of "words on the page" in their minute relations, in their effects of imagery and so on' (Leavis, F. R., 1952, p. 200). He established reading as the experience of an individual reader engaging with an individual artist's work. The aim was to examine the text as a discrete work, to discover truths and experiences which were universal.

Reading was above all a moral activity and texts, properly selected, should be a civilising influence on readers. Of major concern was that a discerning minority should rescue the English heritage and tradition and should, using their finely tuned sensibilities, judge which modern works should pass into that tradition. In turn, the reading of select works would heighten the sensibility of less gifted readers and make them more sensitive to and appreciative of life's finer things. Particular readings of particular texts would create better people. The school's job, then, is one of training the ideal reader to perceive the 'shade, tone and essential structure' of a work whose value has been predetermined. It was also to recognise in the text essential qualities of 'universality' and 'timelessness':

> For if language tends to be debased ... instead of invigorated by contemporary use, then it is to literature alone, where its subtlest and finest use is preserved, that we can look with any hope of keeping in touch with our spiritual tradition – with the 'picked experience of ages'.
>
> (Leavis, F. R., 1933, p. 82)

A major factor underpinning Leavis's argument was his belief in the rightness of the old order. The morality upon which he drew was derived from a nostalgia for what was an allegedly less complex existence. He eschewed theories or systems of analysis and their relevance to literature, returning time and again to the 'individual' and the development of a 'critical inwardness' which would enable the reader to read sensitively and intelligently the words on the page.

As a critical method Structuralism engages with literature as a communicative system, not a mythical creation which transcends scientific analysis. Though a less dominant influence than Leavis on literature teaching in schools, Structuralism at its height offered an alternative to a method of analysis which seemed, certainly in the language it used, to be based entirely on subjective feeling.

Although one of the central premises of structural linguistics is the arbitrary nature of the sign, in the case of linguistics the word, the sign system itself, is not arbitrary. It is dependent on a social system of commonly agreed codes organised according to the principles which order systems and relations within the society itself. The claim of Structuralists is that the text is structured according to literary codes and conventions which are themselves social constructs. The focus for literary analysis, however, is the textual structure itself, not the historical and social context of its making. The reader's task is to decode the text to discover its underlying systems and to see how meaning is made. Structuralist criticism, such as the early work of Barthes, *Writing Degree Zero* (1967), uses the process of decoding to reveal that writing a literary text is not, as was claimed, a reflection of reality; it is not about anything concretely ident- ifiable in the real world, but about itself.

There is an inevitable tension, however, in an analysis which on the one hand identifies the text as a product of social relations while on the other, for the purpose of study, it treats the text as an uncontextualised object. In practice it is sometimes difficult to make a distinct separation between a deep structure which is transcultural and immutable and the sign system, which is historically variant.

In *Literary Theory*, Terry Eagleton claims that it was the 'hard Structuralists', arguing that systems were fixed and beyond cultural difference, who exposed the basic weakness of a Structuralist analysis. He describes it as, 'in a word ... hair raisingly unhistorical':

the laws of the mind it claimed to isolate ... moved at a level of generality quite remote from the concrete differences of human history ... There was no question of relating the work to the realities of which it treated, or to

the conditions which produced it, or the actual readers who studied it ...
(Eagleton, T., 1983, p. 109)

As earlier chapters illustrate, a poem like 'Mi Cyaan Believe It'
raises questions about the nature of language and the social
context of its production; to talk about the language of the
poem would be to look at the historical circumstances in which
languages are produced. An approach to literature which defines
meaning as residing solely in the text excludes literature which
is written, in part, as a conscious opposition to dominant literary
modes. Michael Smith writes in a language which he places in
deliberate opposition to conventional English literary style and
which confirms his distance and alienation from that form. In
an exchange with C. L. R. James (*Arena*, 1983) he consciously
and repeatedly mispronounces 'Shakespeare and Wordsworth':
in that gesture of rebellion he transforms his alienation to
explicit rejection of a tradition from which he would be
excluded.

It is important to state here that his poem is no more the
creation of material – political, cultural and historical – circumstances than, say, *Henry IV* or *The Rainbow*, and there is
no text which is separable from the context of its production.
However, as I will argue more fully in the next chapter, Black
literature signals its materiality more consciously.

In recent years there has been considerable pressure to move
from an approach to literature which involves readers unlocking
the text to reveal meaning and sees interpretation as beyond
the influence of readers' experience. Many teachers, particularly
those not involved in teaching towards the more traditional
examination syllabuses, have adopted a more reader-centred
approach to teaching literature, which allows for the variety of
different experiences students have of reading the text to be expressed. The reason for this change is due, in part at least, to
the influence of the Post-Structuralists and Deconstructionists
on literary criticism. These methods of criticism offer the possi-

bility of breaking with the idea of a unified, whole text, within which meaning is located. Cultures, societies and experience, it is argued, are fragmented, so that there exists neither an 'ideal' closed text nor an 'ideal' reader.

Post-Structuralists stress the multiplicity of meanings produced by different readers' experiences. It is less possible then to invalidate or to exclude a reading or an interpretation. Basing their work on a Structuralist analysis of language, they emphasise not just the arbitrariness of the sign but its emptiness; they thus seek to destroy the idea of 'meaning' in the text, suggested by the term 'signified', arguing that reading is textual production. The text is in fact a signifier which signals endless meanings.

In *S/Z* Barthes decodes the assumption that literature 'reflects' a reality by asserting that literature 'transforms' and structures reality into an image of itself. Literature, which he defines as '*bourgeoise écriture*', structures a reality defined by bourgeois values. He posits the 'mythologist' as opposed to the 'reader' as someone who empties the signs of their signified; who sees in the text a system of signifying codes which are reconstructions of the 'real'. The reader's task, then, is not to determine traditional, agreed or even intended meanings, but to produce the meaning of the text. The 'ideal' text possesses a 'galaxy' of signifiers:

> It has no beginning, it is reversible; we gain access to it by several entrances, none of which can be authoritatively declared to be the main one; the codes it mobilizes extend as far as the eye can reach; they are indeterminable.
>
> (Barthes, R., *S/Z*, p. 5)

What Barthes had signalled was the death of the author; this would have marked the end of questions about authorial intent and the idea of the author as an individual authoritative voice.

Titles of such articles as 'Stories that Readers Tell' (Protherough, 1987) and 'Readers Re-creating Texts' (Evans, 1987) establish the reader's role as central to the production of meaning. As these titles imply, reading is an active process of interaction between reader and text. Meaning is made when the reader engages with the text by bringing her experiences of life, of reading and of other narratives, to a reconstruction of the text itself. The result is a shift in the balance of power within a classroom discourse; the reader no longer assists the student in arriving at a correct interpretation but facilitates the production of a multiplicity of meanings.

'Dialogue with a Text' (Probst, 1988) is the account of a teacher entering a classroom, prepared to 'conduct a recitation on the three techniques of characterisation'. The students, however, had been prompted, by the text, to explore their own lives, fears and ambitions. As the writer explains, if he had allowed the students to express a truly individual response, they would as readers have been engaging with real thought rather than a 'recall of term and definitions.'

There have been criticisms of an approach to teaching literature which allows as many responses to flourish as there are readers, from traditional educationalists and from others, like Pam Gilbert (1987), whose reservations about these critical methods are that they do not take into account the social and political construction of literature and of readers. There is also, as she observes, the danger of chaos resulting from the production of, for example, a classroom of thirty meanings which are 'totally personal and therefore totally plural'. In practice there are institutional checks such as assessment, or there are attempts at some form of consensus within the classroom context which might militate against this.

She questions whether, as criticism of Leavis has shown, the term 'personal' is not in fact being used to describe a response which is learnt. Students learn to use a language which is personal to describe an interpretation which, however unintentionally, the teacher has authorised.

There are further constraints on the production of a truly 'personal' response. Literary texts are not on the whole accessible to inexperienced readers; in practice, therefore, the teacher's role becomes one of opening up the text and making it more meaningful to students: reading a text in an environment which validates it, determines, and serves to control readers' experience of reading, and the meanings they make.

Eagleton takes an analysis of the 'personal' much further, arguing that in relation to literature, 'personal', as in 'personal response', is used as an entirely abstract term. Yet, as he reminds us, all personal life is 'determined by a wider public one'. All subjects are created within a political, historical and cultural context. Further, literature as a form reinforces the separation of the individual from society and thus acts as a method of social and political control. He defines literature as 'a form of moral technology':

> a particular set of techniques and practices for the instilling of specific kinds of value, discipline, behaviour and response in human subjects ...
>
> (Eagleton, T., 1985, p. 5)

The study of literature produces a specific type of subject, one that is 'sensitive, creative, imaginative' about 'nothing in particular'. The purpose of reading a literary text is to acquire these qualities and become a richer human being – an end in itself. A reader is trained to be 'sensitive', but that experience of reading and responding does not motivate change or prompt action. He uses the example of a reading of *King Lear* and argues that the although the play 'urges solidarity with the oppressed', to interpret it in that way, to offer that as a 'personal response', would not be acceptable as valid literary criticism.

Black writing is, as I have argued, expressly political. However, it functions within a discourse which actively seeks to depoliticise and abstract texts from their wider historical and political contexts. As a result, the reader is often caught in an uncomfortable wedge of contradiction – as is the case, for example, when watching South African drama in the context of a well-furnished theatre, and as part of an audience which is economically comfortable and politically secure. The plays themselves contain explicit images of oppression, of sacrifice, and often urge revolutionary action. It could be argued, however, that the discourse in which such a play is placed prevents it from being interpreted as a literal call to arms, or action of any sort; that the audience, well trained in sensitive and imaginative response, interprets its message, in Eagleton's phrase, 'experientially and personally'. They leave, having become emotionally enriched by the experience; they are moved, but only in relation to the drama.

It is often the case, as with Black writing, that the distinction between the literary and the political is challenged. The example in Chapter 1 of a student asking, after reading 'Frankie Mae', whether the teacher wants her to hate white people is illustrative of this, though it could be argued that such a response is possible only from 'untrained' readers. However, many Black readers do perceive the role of Black writers as central to a community's political life and most, possibly all, Black writers do engage with that question – either in the work itself, or as a subject of constant debate among writers and readers. Political discourse within the literature itself is often read seriously by those whose power it questions; Ngugi, for example, was detained for his fictional work and because of his involvement in the Literature Department of the University, and in prison he was warned by a warder not to write 'poems' while in detention.

There is, among literature teachers, a movement towards approaches to reading as discourse; approaches which place centrally the social, historical and cultural context of readers and texts. Some of this analysis – Richard Exton's 'The Post-Structuralist Always Reads Twice' (1982), for example – is developed as one of the possibilities within Deconstructionist criticism, while other work is more clearly defined as 'political' or 'materialist' criticism and is developed in response to the perceived lack of a material base to Post-Structuralist analysis.

While criticising the tendency to anti-historicism in the Post-

Structuralist, materialist critics such as Peter Brookner and Tony Bennett point out the significance of critics such as Barthes, Derrida and in particular, Foucault and Lacan of a more ideological theory of literature. As anti-essentialists they challenge the cultural ideology which enshrines 'truth' in the texts of the canon. The text, argues Derrida (1966), yields:

> an extending, unrepresented plurality of meanings [. . .] produced not by the intentions or creativity of the author.   (In Bennett, Tony, 1982, pp. 226/7)

Meaning is not the preserve of an ideal reader, or of an author. As the students' reading of 'Calypso' suggests, meaning is produced through a complex interaction between experience and circumstance and the context in which the reading takes place. My initial question causes the class to focus on calypso and to explore for themselves the meaning and function of that art form in relation to both themselves and the poem. Its significance to the poem is explored more fully than I could have counted on in a reading of my own.

Another example of the way in which students' readings can subvert notions of fixed meanings, on which so much literature teaching depends, is illustrated by the reading of *Henry IV* by an Eritrean student in my literature class. Aziz questioned my assessment of the king as humane, forgiving and peace-loving. Despite his past actions, I said, he desired a peaceful and harmonious country. Aziz pointed out that no king contemplating the slaugher of Muslims over territory which was theirs and in which they lived could be described in such terms, highlighting the way in which religion and morality (the rationale for the Crusades) are used to justify imperialist design. Teachers like myself tend to opt for the safe interpretation, validated by the tradition and reproduced in the form of examination questions and notes at the back of the book. Having been trained as an 'ideal reader' I could never have produced so vital an interpretation as either of these at eighteen. Now I am as confident as my students whom the system has failed;

and coming back to the text after fifteen years, I started at the opening scene of *Henry IV* for the same reasons as Aziz – yet I wasn't confident enough, as a teacher working in the school system, to encourage students like him to produce and develop his own meaning in an examination.

What needs to be stressed, as this example shows, is the social positioning of the reader in relation to the text. Dave Morley (1980) argues that the abstractness and non-specificity of the Post-Structuralist position means that as an analysis it does not give central importance to social and historical relations. Subjects, he argues, are formed within discursive practices which continually operate on them. The subject's position in relation to the text is determined by the context of writers' actions. Readers need to take into account the text's function within a particular historical moment and within particular cultures or institutions. The individual subject is shaped by race, class and gender and by additional discourse within each of these categories. The language of the text and the text itself are ideological constructs. Critics such as Morley would argue, however, that this context should be the basis of critical methods – not, as in a Post-Structuralist analysis, another discourse made possible by the text's plurality.

In 'Text and History' Tony Bennett asserts that meaning is not produced only in the discursive strategies of the text. The 'readings' which produce a plurality of meaning must constitute social activity. He focuses on Derrida's use of 'materiality' and uses it to mean material in the political sense of being produced in actual relations:

> There is no text that is accessible behind or beyond the different forms in which its historical existence is modulated. (Bennett, Tony, 1982, p. 234)

Before the 'reading' of the text, there is the important factor of its production: how and why it appears as a literary text. Educational institutions, the media and social and economic forces determine the intellectual spirit of the age and its literature, which either challenges or reflects it:

> The text does not occupy a position but is always and forever installed in
> a field of struggle, mobilized, placed, positioned and articulated with other
> texts in different ways within different critical practices, which, sometimes
> obliquely, sometimes directly, themselves play into and register within
> neighbouring areas of ideological struggle.   (ibid., p. 229)

Bakhtin's theory of language as social discourse, as communication, has influenced approaches to criticism which are 'political'. In opposition to a Structuralist theory of language as an abstract system, he argues that the basis of all language is interactive. He describes communication as essential to being; conversation or dialogue as the first learned language and the basis of all language. The 'self' is social and we encounter ourselves in languages, the voices spoken by others. A language is a whole system of meanings, expressing the contradictions of any society, and in the same way that society is not a monolith of structures, language is not a fixed system of meanings: the voice of the speaker is therefore not the voice of a distinct individual but one which is produced in various discourses.

Literature as a form, he argues, communicates particularly a set of values. The form, however, is composed of a 'multiplicity of styles' in their constant echoing or, more specifically, as the word involved in 'dialogue'. Behind each reply stands a speaker; therefore the word in the novel is always socially charged, and necessarily polemical.

Tony Davies gives an example of the way in which the language of a novel is 'socially charged and polemical' and the way in which ideal reading or criticism imposes unity and coherence on the contradiction and the gaps. He writes: 'the relationship between literature and literary language is as contradictory as the "nation" in "national" language' (Davies, Tony, 1980, p. 11). Using *The Mill on the Floss* as an example, he argues that, although it has been criticised for having a 'weak ending', a 'coherent', neat ending would have been impossible and is in any case irrelevant, given the contradictions inherent in its writing. It is written by a woman, disguised as a man in the language of the dominant tradition, yet it offers a critique of the sexual and educational exploitation of the lower middle classes. The activity of reading the contradictions as part of the text is constrained by the need to resolve, in an 'ideal' reading, textual conflict. Further disjunctions arise from the production of the text in schools where students are being asked to read in a language which is described as theirs but which they do not identify with. The language of the text enters the context of the classroom as a contested form and reading ceases to be a passive activity.

'Re-reading' in itself, though useful and necessary, is not enough if teachers and critics are still functioning within an authorised canon and not questioning its most basic assumptions. 'Re-readings' may become used as ways of reaffirming the text's timelessness, its adaptability to new historical contexts and its universal relevance. In forms of criticism which are, as Bennett writes, 'forms of activity inseparable from the wider social relations between reader and writer', exists the potential to change both what is taught in schools as literature and how it is taught. This would mean that different forms of literature have equal access to and status in the curriculum; that special categories do not have to be formulated for literature which seems overtly political. This would create the space necessary for a questioning of assumptions about 'human experience' and about what is natural and who is human.

Such a change of emphasis in an approach to the study of literature is being made necessary by the fact that the population of many inner-city schools and colleges is changing. Far more of the students we are teaching are not English and there is pressure from students, teachers and from within the community to change the curriculum and to develop educational practices which are more appropriate to a changed school, social and political environment.

The value of Black literature to English teaching is that it does force students, who read it alongside other texts, to question the form and nature of both Black literature itself and traditional English literature. This however, can occur only if the full extent of the challenge it offers is acknowledged and understood.

7

'New World, New Words'

and when we speak we are afraid
our words will not be heard
nor welcomed
but when we are silent
we are still afraid
So it is better to speak
remembering we were not meant to survive
(from 'A Litany for Survival', Audré Lorde)

It is unstated, though evident from the English curriculum of
schools and colleges, that the study of 'literature' refers to the
study of texts by white, mainly European authors. There may
be added further specifications, which denote form, period,
geography, or a national identity; nineteenth-century French
literature, for example, narrows the area of study, but the
cultural boundaries defined by the term 'literature' are clear.
'Black' literature is so defined because it is different from (white)
literature. It is neither a description of form nor of location,
but is used cross-culturally and cross-nationally to describe,
inclusively, African writing in English, French, Portuguese or
Swahili; Caribbean writing, literature by non-white writers in
Britain, and so on. The difference is one which is created and
perpetuated by the selectivity of the literary establishment and
its 'tradition', and it is one which is exploited by Black writers
themselves. The distinction is used by Black writers who use

the term to describe their own work, to challenge that 'tradition'. It then becomes literature produced in opposition to an excluding and exclusive canon. In that sense it is polemical; created out of a supposed silence and the absence of a literary tradition and speaking of the struggle and conflict which form the material context of its production. It presents a challenge to critical methods which abstract meaning from the text, and to literary institutions which apply culturally selective criteria to define what is or isn't literature.

Black culture is constantly in a process of being remade and redefined, after whole bodies of culture, evidence of a people's existence, have been destroyed. The struggle to create bodies of literature, even to write after cultures have been literally 'written off', is reflected in the contradictions and tensions in the language, form and subject matter of the text. Literary production becomes an expression of being, politically and culturally. Black writers constantly demonstrate an explicit consciousness that the process in which they are engaged is both creative and political. This is particularly evident in writing during the post-colonial period in Africa and the Caribbean.

Aimé Césaire, speaking at the conference of Negro African writers in 1956, said:

> We find ourselves today in cultural chaos. And this is our role; to liberate the forces which alone can organize from this chaos a new synthesis ...
>
> We are here to proclaim the right of our people to speak ...
>
> (*Nobody Knows My Name*, Baldwin, 1961, p.40)

The conference was for writers and artists, and its objective was to discuss the creative process. Many of the writers present were both producers of literature and, like Léopold Senghor and Aimé Césaire, politicians, or people who were involved in the formation of a political and national identity. Inevitably the political context of their work was never far from the discussion, and in some cases dominated the contributions. The struggle to emerge from colonialism and to forge a cultural identity which incorporated all aspects of that history was central to Césaire's speech. It would involve piecing together a past that had been destroyed and reclaiming it. It would also, he argued somewhat ironically, involve support for the emergence of an 'active, living culture', whose basis would be in the community and would be formed out of the experiences of the 'masses'. He clearly implies that cultural production by elite minorities does not represent the culture of the people, and he refuses, intellectually at least, to identify with an elitist 'subculture', confined to an existence on the margin allowed it by European culture. In 1946 he became the Deputy to the French National Assembly for Martinique and the Mayor of Fort de France, Martinique's capital.

Like many writers in the Caribbean and Africa, the strong cultural influences which are inescapable features of his own development as writer and statesman are reflected in his writing. Educated out of the peasant, and still very African, culture of his parents into a select school in Martinique's capital, he followed the traditional route of the 'assimilationist' into the Ecole Normale Supérieure in Paris. The contradictory nature of this process – the fact that it was to take place in a deeply hostile environment – resulted in Césaire, and others like him from the French colonies studying in Paris during the thirties, espousing an ideology which contained a complete rejection of Western cultural values. His early work, *Return to My Native Land*, is an artistic expression of the political and cultural philosophy, Negritude, which evolved during that period and is a conscious part of a revolutionary re-examination of cultural forms and values. The work is a reinterpretation of colonial and European modes of being and expression. It challenges terms such as 'civilisation' and exposes it as a synonym for oppression and conquest. Exorcising the past with images of violence, he creates a new paradigm of human and humane values. He asserts African culture where there is silence and negation and celebrates its existence and its achievements.

The lines

> Heia for the royal Kailcedrate!
> Heia for those who have never invented anything
> those who have never explored anything
> who have never tamed anything . . .

though seeming to embrace a romantic ideal of the 'noble savage', are in fact a symbol of that process of re-creation. And to assert the validity of a culture which has been so negated is to question the norms defined by the dominant, excluding culture.

There is in the poem strong symbolist imagery. He uses a European literary form to maximum effect to undermine the traditional conventions of language as a form and to question 'form'. The synthesis of cultures, which in his work are presented as oppositional, is not exploited explicitly by Césaire; for other Caribbean writers like Brathwaite, however, it is a creative dynamic which is central to his work.

The form that much Black writing takes, particularly in Africa and the Caribbean, is a reflection of the contradictory wedge in which Black writers are placed. Many writers are, like Césaire, educated in a language and into a culture which is overtly antagonistic to the language and culture of the masses within their societies. Yet out of that potentially elitist and marginal subculture of 'mimic men' a literary form emerges which, containing all the ironies of that experience, subverts and challenges both the dominant culture and the subculture from which the writers are formed.

The seeming lack of unity and resolution in form and the apparent specificity of the text have meant that in terms of traditional literary criticism, Black literature is seen as deficient. It would be 'literature', it is said, if it could overcome its contradictions and particularities and address 'human' concerns.

The struggle to create a Caribbean cultural identity dominated the work of many Caribbean writers in the twenty years before the first islands became independent, although colonial influences persist in much of the writing of this period. Less evident – and Césaire stands out in this respect from the work of English-speaking Caribbean writers – is a search for identity, directed towards Africa. There is instead a consciousness of the metropolitan culture's superiority and a doubt that a 'West Indian' culture exists. George Lamming's *The Pleasures of Exile* is a discussion of the problem of being part of elite, consciously marginal or 'peripheral' culture within the wider context of West Indian culture. Although the group of writers to which he refers do in their writing depict the culture of the majority of rural peasants or urban poor and in that sense can be seen to be responding to 'an active living' culture and, therefore, being in some ways a part of its making, the writers themselves most definitely represent a distinct subculture of intellectuals caught between that culture and the culture of their education. As novelists and poets, Lamming claims, West Indian writers in the 1950s had no indigenous audience. They write of a culture which they could perhaps have claimed to have shared as young boys, but the form of cultural expression is European and, it might be said, is written for a European audience. Lamming would argue that this is in part due to the fact that those within the emerging national bourgeoisie, who were assuming political and intellectual leadership, were actively uninterested in any form of artistic expression which reflected the culture of the region. As a result, the logical step for writers and artists was to move into the 'home' of the culture within which they had been nurtured:

> every one of them, Mittelholzer, Reid, Mais, Selvon, Hearne, Carew, Naipaul, Andrew Salkey, Neville Dawes, everyone has felt the need to get out.   (Lamming, George, 1960, p.41)

It is disturbing that colonial dominance is so thorough that regardless of whether it is, like the French policy of assimilation, explicitly stated or otherwise, the effect of stripping communities of any form of cultural identity is equally complete. Lamming's book is in part an attempt to investigate that process.

He writes of colonialism in the Caribbean:

> It is not merely a political definition; it is not merely the result of certain economic arrangements. It started as these, and grew somewhat deeper. Colonialism is the very base and structure of the West Indian's Cultural awareness.   (ibid., p.35)

As if attesting to the truth of his own analysis, in three substantial sections of his work Lamming explores extensively the symbolic dynamic between Prospero and Caliban. He presents a fairly conventional analysis of *The Tempest* and then, in a later section – 'Caliban Orders History' – extends the relationship, using Caliban actually to usurp Prospero's power. He posits Caliban as the rebellious slave who, using the same tools – language and culture – with which Prospero has endowed him, breaks his control, defeats him and wins independence.

By using Prospero and Caliban to represent the coloniser and the colonised, however, Lamming tacitly accepts the distinction between the two. Prospero is the embodiment of European civilised culture, possessed of a benevolent magic, wisdom and, most importantly, language. He 'tames' and controls Caliban the slave: the embodiment of evil sorcery and mute ignorance. Unlike Césaire he does not assert, in however romanticised a form, beauty in the 'beast', but retains, in his own flight from the text, the correlation between slave and savage.

He confirms Prospero's 'gift' of language as just that:

> Prospero has given Caliban language and with an unstated history of consequences an unknown history of future intentions. It is this way, entirely Prospero's enterprise, which makes Caliban aware of possibilities.
> (Lamming, George, 1960, p.41)

So when Lamming's Caliban, the African slave, as Toussaint L'Ouverture, revolts successfully and heroically, it hardly matters, since everything he has become is due to Prospero. It is Prospero's 'enterprise' to provide him with the tools of his (Prospero's) own destruction, therefore Caliban's victory is not really his own, but Prospero's.

Caliban has become an important symbol, to Caribbean writers, of colonialism in the Caribbean. The Shakespearian characteristics of lechery and drunkenness within the form of the ignorant savage are retained, regardless of whether these are used to reflect negatively on the master/colonizer. David Dabydeen, in his recent *Coolie Odyssey*, explores the same dynamic, but within the clear confines of the given relationship. The Black man, after a drunken evening, makes love to Miranda. She uses him to indulge her own fantasies, while he offers no resistance:

> Fashioning me your Image or casting me Native
> White woman, womb of myth, foundry or funeral pyre
> where like a Hindu corpse I burn and shrink
> To be reborn to your desire . . .
>
> (Dabydeen, David, 1988, p.34)

Her indifference and control contrast starkly with his naiveté and his total abandon to sensuous pleasure: she leaves 'crisply':

> Whilst I, coiled blackly within myself,
> Paralysed with rage and wonder,
> straining still to sense your presence,
> Craving still the magic of your making.
>
> (ibid., p.34)

'Caliban' is in one sense the object of her desire, her creation: in relation to him she is more powerful, more confident of the system of cultural codes within which they operate. For his part, however, he is entranced, caught and controlled. There is no contest.

Unsettling though the persistence of 'Calibanism' may be, it is evidence that one of the legacies of colonialism is the colonial imagination. Nowhere, perhaps, has the process of colonisation been more complete than in the Caribbean. It would therefore be unrealistic and critically unconstructive to expect a successful rejection of 'Caliban' and the attendant images of savagery and inferiority.

Rather than accepting that the literature is a mimicry of

European forms, the marginal creation of a marginal culture, Brathwaite, in his autobiographical article 'Timerhi', argues that Caribbean literature is a valid form, created out of the cultural 'chaos' of that society. It is, he states, a 'plural' society, one which is culturally fragmented. Further displacement occurs at the level of class; educated writers and readers:

> start out in the world without a sense of 'wholeness'. Identification with any one of these orientations can only consolidate the concept of a plural society, a plural vision ... Disillusion with the fragmentations leads to a sense of rootlessness ... the result: dislocation of the sensibility.
>
> (Brathwaite, Kamau, 1970, p.36)

Reflections of this plurality are found in the works of Naipaul, C. L. R. James, George Lamming – in fact, most Caribbean writers.

Of his own experience, Brathwaite writes:

> The day the first snow fell I floated to my birth, of feathers falling by my window   (*Other Exiles*, 1975, p.7)

The cultural references of his education had been, it seemed at the time, more powerful than his own culture and his actual lived experience. As a young boy growing up in Barbados he felt distanced from his community and environment. Even though he actually participated in that community he identified with a remote metropolis. The role played by a colonial education in validating a sense of what was worthwhile was immense. Many years later, he commented:

> And in terms of what we write, our perceptual modes, we are more conscious (in terms of sensibility) of the falling snow ... than the force of the hurricane which takes place every year.
>
> (*The History of the Voice*, 1984, p.8)

When he embraced the culture of the north, of the snow, as if it were his own, however, and celebrated it in iambic pentameters, his Cambridge colleagues rejected it, preferring instead a poetic expression of his home, a place and culture from which he was so alienated that his own writings about that place and time seemed to him to have an exotic flavour. That

kind of alienation through rejection and through the inability
to perceive valid cultural forms in one's own experience is the
kind of cultural complexity that I tried to explore in the first
chapter, and one in which Black students find themselves.

Brathwaite 'returned' – accidentally in fact, since Africa did
not feature in his consciousness as a place with which he had
any cultural connection – to Ghana, where he 'repossessed' the
aboriginal culture of Africa:

> The middle passage had now guessed its end. The connection between my
> lived but unheeded non-middle-class boyhood and its Great Tradition on
> the Eastern mainland had been made ...   ('Timerhi', 1970, p.38)

Despite the 'connection' and 'repossessing', the plural vision
remains inherent in the form. It is a constituent of Black writing
in European languages. A poem like 'Calypso' is an example of
this where, among the complex patterns of ironies, are the
historical relationships of the languages and forms in the poem
itself.

X-Self, Brathwaite's latest collection of poems, represents his
most uncompromising attempt so far to confront and exploit
the contradictory tension within his own work. The reader no
longer needs to comb the text to see the residual colonial
reference or tone. Here it is incorporated into the form. He
describes the work as the cultural and literary representation of
'Caribbean Man': 'i-man/caribbean — and multifarious with
the learning and education that this implies' (Brathwaite,
Kamau, 1987, p.113).

The plural culture of the Caribbean is transformed through
the poem to become multilayered and multidimensional. The
effect is prismatic, reflecting endless possibilities and meanings,
of reference and cross-reference. He probes beyond the token,
popular symbols of African cultures and incorporates into his
work gods, ritual and symbolic systems which are unreclaimed
features of his ancestral heritage. More revolutionary are his
incursions into Central and South American cultures, to which
the original 'Caribbean man' belonged.

It would be to overstate the case to argue that this fractured past and present form a straightforward 'whole' in all the major works of Caribbean writers. It is important, however, to stress that the contradictions, which are the result of the sometimes conflicting or even opposing cultural forms within the writing itself, do not invalidate the text. They do not represent aspects of a 'developing' form or of 'emerging' artistic consciousness, but are elements of the form itself. The work is self-conscious and is often implicitly or explicitly about the ironies and gaps within the cultural contexts of its own production.

Unlike in the Caribbean, where it seems that an impetus towards critical debate has stagnated, particularly in the years since 'dub poetry' came to prominence in Jamaica and disturbed notions about literary language and creativity, in Africa literary criticism flourishes. The debate concerning an 'African' cultural identity, the nature of literary production and the kinds of tools needed for productive, progressive criticism has become increasingly vigorous. There are many trends, strands and positions in the debate. While it is crude and inaccurate to talk of an 'African' tradition of literature and literary criticism, it is impossible to enter a discourse without using already determined prescriptions and definitions. It is important, however, to admit their limitations and to emphasise that the 'traditions' referred to here derive, in the main, from West Africa.

In an interesting study, which charts the evolution of the novel in Nigeria, J. P. O'Flinn (1975) attempts to account for the massive popularity of novels such as Achebe's *Things Fall Apart* and *A Man of the People*. He argues that while the novel was the production of a very small elitist class, that class – the national bourgeoisie – expressed for a brief period during the post-independence years the aspirations of the whole country. He attributes that coincidence of interest to the success of the early Nigerian novel.

Using Achebe as an example, he contrasts the popularity of his early novels with his silence during the civil war period.

Achebe himself distinguishes the two periods by describing a changed consciousness. He recognised that the whole culture of Nigeria was undergoing a traumatic change, and that the protagonists in that process were different from those who had sought to change and determine Nigeria's path to independence. As a writer he felt that his own relationship to the economic, cultural and political context of Nigeria itself had to adjust accordingly. The 'bourgeois intelligentsia' no longer had a role in the turmoil of the civil war years and was no longer suited to meet the challenges of a new era. He could no longer, from that position, pretend that he had anything to offer his country's development – a role which, it is implied, is inextricably bound in his task as a writer:

> the culture of a people is more than books and poems ... while the intellectual was obviously displaying the past cultures of Africa, the troubled peoples of Africa were already creating new revolutionary cultures which took into account their present conditions
>
> (Chinua Achebe in O'Flinn, 1975, pp.49/50)

Here, he is clearly describing the function of his early novels: they had presented a cultural stasis, and writers in Nigeria had still felt that it was their role to revive the past and to represent pre-colonial African cultures and traditions. The artist, according to Achebe, had 'been left far behind the people who make culture ...'

He continues:

> I can write poetry – something short, intense, more in keeping with my mood. I can write essays. I can even lecture. All this is creating in the context of our struggle ... I wouldn't consider writing a poem on daffodils particularly creative in my situation now
>
> (Chinua Achebe in O'Flinn, 1976, pp.17, 18)

Recognition of the ideology and practices which have produced Black forms of writing has led radical African critics like Chinweizu, one of the most stridently contemptuous critics of the tendency to judge African writing against European literary forms, to state that African novels can be read only in a social and political context.

He is prescriptive in his argument: he exhorts African writers to maintain an African cultural identity and to shed 'all encrustations of a colonial mentality'. It is interesting that his call to Africans to rehabilitate and repossess our past echoes Brathwaite's journey and his reconnection to an African cultural tradition. With writers like Senghor (1961) he argues that an understanding or a criticism of African literature must take into account the significance of the political, social and historical circumstances of the text's production. Senghor claims that in Africa the division between art and life does not exist; hence the concept of 'art for art's sake' is one which has been grafted on to African culture and does not describe the culture of the majority of Africans, for whom art is functional, perishable and remade each time the work is destroyed. Despite the influence of traditional forms and functions of African art on modern African writing, the 'African novel' does not belong to traditional forms of culture, but is the creation of a contradictory interrelation of European culture and an indigenous culture. Nevertheless, writes Chinweizu, it is an African-based form, and because it is written in English should not be treated by critics as if it were an 'overseas department of the Great Canon'.

If Black writing is to be read as it defines itself, then where does it stand in relation to European literary 'tradition'? Chinweizu and Irele would argue that to continue with reference to a tradition at all would be to negate the value of African writing and African cultural traditions. Irele argues for a 'sociological' reading of African literature, based in the political and social context of African society. He writes, extending this approach to a reading of all literature, 'I consider that literature has no meaning detached from the feelings of the people whom it represents' (*The African Experience in Literature and Ideology*, 1981, p.40).

To use a 'sociological' approach teaching only Black literature may be damaging in the context of schools. It could confirm the 'outsider' status of that literature and it would also be to deny that in its particularity it expresses central human experiences. A reading of Black literature which treats as crucial the context of the text's production cannot sit alongside an idealised reading of the great tradition.

There is a powerful argument against the 'sociologisation', of Black literature, which is how Irele can sometimes be interpreted. Gates (1984), Brathwaite (1984) and African critics such as Iyasere (1975), Anozie (1984) argue that Black literature has been read as an illumination of the sociological and economic problems or crisis in Black communities and that this has been at the expense of a close reading of the text and an analysis of textual structures. Gates, in *Black Literature and Literary Theory*, describes it as the 'anthropology' fallacy, and continues:

> Our list could be extended to include all sorts of concerns with the possible *functions* of *Black* texts in non-literary arenas rather than with their internal structures as acts of language or their formal status as works of art.
>
> (Gates, L., 1985, p.5)

His concern is to establish a Black tradition, with the aim of providing a foundation for a literary canon. Sheer 'chaos', he admits, has been created within the existing canon by the cultural production of Black writers; he recognises that the terms of reference for the English tradition, and the criteria for inclusion of canonical works, have been used less as a framework for critical analysis than as a mechanism of political control. The difficulty with this argument, however, is that the establishment of a separate tradition does not guarantee equal status with works of the 'great tradition'. As with most separate but equal policies, it provides a structure for institutionalised inequality and discrimination.

Gates does not deny that the political and historical struggles to create are integral to the creative form of Black texts. In fact, the example he gives of close analysis of language structures within the text is illustrative of this:

The Afro-American tradition has been figurative from its beginning. How could it have survived otherwise? Black people have always been masters of the figurative: saying one thing to mean quite another has been basic to Black survival in oppressive Western cultures.   (ibid., p.6)

It is vital, he argues, to be aware of this tradition of 'figuration' and the way in which it is expressed both linguistically and in the form and structure of the text. However, this is not to see the text itself as 'merely' a tool of struggle: it is formed in that context but has a separate identity – that is, as a discrete work of art. He argues for a close reading – a method which recognises that the text reflects a range of cultural and literary influences, but abstracts the work from its context for analytical purposes and does not use the text to validate a particular ideological and cultural position. In his critical method, Gates uses the means of Western traditions of criticism but to a different end, one shaped by the differences in the work of art itself.

There are tensions among critics who would broadly agree with this position. There is a tendency, as Appiah (1984) argues in a critique of the use of Structuralist analysis in relation to African literature, to prove that the worth of the writing lies in the fact that these critical methods can be applied successfully with comparable, but not identical results. This he sees as part of the process of 'justifying' the culture; if it needs to be 'justified' then Black critics are still looking from a position of inferiority in relation to the 'tradition'. The test for the inclusion of a text in a Black tradition would always therefore be its measure in relation to European literary values. While Appiah does not actually criticise Structuralism as a critical method, nor its use in relation to African texts, he does object to using it to standardise the text and to fit works into a culturally defined set of literary criteria. This he describes as:

the post-colonial legacy which requires us to show that African literature is worthy of study precisely (but only) because it is fundamentally the same as European literature.   (ibid., p.145)

The argument for close reading, or for the use of a critical method which gives priority to a close analysis of the text independently of its context, raises many complex and difficult issues, particularly when examining approaches to the teaching of Black literary texts as part of a broad literature curriculum, and not as a discrete body. Gates is concerned with 'value', and it cannot be denied that this is important. What seems to be counterproductive is the use of canonical criteria as the measure of 'value'. Rather, Black literary production should be used to expose as limitations the selective criteria of the established literary canon.

The marginalisation of writing by Black writers, writers who are not part of the traditions of the dominant culture and whom that culture has actively suppressed and negated, has, ironically, exposed the limitations of the values on which criticism rests. The terms 'universality' and 'human truths', standards by which texts are judged, prove irrelevant when used in relation to non-white texts. They can be applied to white, male, middle-class experience, but by implicit definition they exclude most other experience. The process of exclusion involves the use of criteria such as 'universality' to justify the claim that the content of Black writing is culturally specific and therefore relevant only to a narrow readership. The fact that the term cannot be employed to describe a range of cultural experiences, however, reflects the inadequacy of the term itself, not of the texts which cannot be incorporated into this definition.

Criticism which marginalises takes different forms, but the basic proposition is the same: Black writing will be 'literature' when it no longer limits itself to the histories and experiences of Black people. There is, in fact, a tradition of this kind of criticism. Anthony Sampson's welcome to Peter Abraham's book *A Wreath for Udomo* (in *The Observer*), is an example:

> It is a dispassionate, critical book without the bitterness of self pity that obscures much African writing. Here thank goodness is an African book which is not all about race ...   (Sampson, A., 1956)

Another is Sara Blackburn, described by Barbara Smith as a 'putative feminist', who, in a review of *Sula*, writes:

> Toni Morrison is far too talented to remain only a marvellous recorder of the Black side of provincial American life ...
>
> (Smith, B. in Showalter, E. (ed.), 1986, p.171)

All Black writers function within a literary discourse which either defines them as 'absent/Black', not white, or as present, but 'other'. Rather than adopting a strategic pose of supplication, of banging on the great canonical door waiting to be let in, Black writers, as earlier illustrations have shown, are creating a tradition, in its non-selective sense, of writing which is both different and challenging.

The most radical articulation of this challenge has come from Black women writers and critics. Recent (1988) interviews with Toni Morrison are illustrative of this. The publication of her latest novel, *Beloved*, was followed by a critical storm. Black writers used a full page of the *New York Times* to award her the recognition she and generations of other Black writers had been denied. The entire interchange between those writers and the literary establishment exposed the politically and culturally partisan nature of the prize-giving establishment, particularly.

Toni Morrison herself has always defended the integrity of the Black writer and argued for the right to self-definition – the right to maintain that integrity:

> And let's put the record straight;
> I am merely, solely additionally,
> however you want to put it: a black
> woman writer ...
> Writing is about danger for me:
> it's like life – you can go under,
> like all art it has to be political and it
> has to be beautiful ...
>
> (Morrison, T., in *Spare Rib*, April 1988, p.15)

Barbara Christian elaborates on the nature of the challenge. She describes the implications for traditional notions of literature when generations of women who were the dusters and cleaners in great libraries write, and when their writing is talked about. In their writing, and their articulation of a cultural reality which has hitherto been invalidated, lies the potential for revolutionary approaches to literature and our reading of it.

Christian radically overturns the subversion of Black working-class women's experience, which she describes as the most 'common' experience in the world. That experience should be used to subvert all judgements by the minority – white bourgeois males – that their literature and culture contain representations of universal, human truths. She describes the established opposition to any literature which does not reflect the values of this powerful minority:

> When this literature is not neglected, it is denigrated by the use of labels that deny its centrality to American life. It is called 'political', 'social protest' or 'minority literature', which in this ironic country has a pejorative sound meaning it lacks craft and has not transcended the limitations of racial, sexual or class boundaries – that it supposedly does not do what 'good' literature does: express our universal humanity.
>
> (Christian, Barbara, 1985, p.160)

She continues:

> And it is precisely because this literature reveals a basic truth of all societies that it is central. In every other society where there is 'other' ... the 'other' struggles to declare the truth and therefore create the truth in forms that exist for her or him. The creation of that truth also changes the perception of those who believe that they are the norm.   (ibid.)

While the material context of canonical texts remains unacknowledged there will always be a distinction between literature which is 'great' and expresses 'truth' and that which is temporary, whose truths are culturally specific. Such is the importance of this distinction in the teaching of English that my Further Education students – the subjects of this book – who have barely been within reach of the canon understand (perfectly) the selective function of the tradition.

In the process of contextualising Black texts, therefore, we must be aware – and ensure that our students are aware – that contexts need to be provided for all literary texts. In other words, we consciously need to acknowledge that we place all texts in the world, and that in our classification of literary production and our approaches to teaching we signal the historical, social and cultural context of its making. No teacher would approach Shakespeare without some reference to the historical context of his work and its means of production, yet we still speak of its timelessness and 'truths' as though the writing had been an idealised rather than a concrete activity.

Although Black literature represents a powerful challenge to those claims, we cannot assume that it will automatically reveal basic 'human truths'; opposition to its existence as 'literature' is continuous, changing and powerful. The task for teachers and educationalists is to ensure that Black writing is valued critically; that it is read as it defines itself, as a cultural and artistic whole reflecting and a reflection of the political and cultural struggles which are its context. The reading should not be used to confirm its status as 'other' but to 'change the perceptions' of the minority who are the gate-keepers of the canon and who have defined 'human' in terms of their own image.

Bibliography

Abrahams, Peter, *A Wreath for Udomo* (1956) Faber.

Achebe, Chinua, *Things Fall Apart* (1958) Heinemann.

Achebe, Chinua, *Arrow of God* (1964) Heinemann.

Alvarado, S., 'Reading and Race', *The English Magazine*, 3 (1980).

Anozie, Sunday O. 'Negritude, structuralism: deconstruction' in Gates (1984).

Appiah, Anthony, 'Strictures on structures: the prospects for a structuralist poetics of African fiction' in Gates (1984).

Baker, Houston A., Jr. (ed.), *Reading Black: Essays in the Criticism of African, Caribbean and Black American Literature* (1976) Cornell University.

Baldwin, James, *Another Country* (1962; Corgi, 1965).

Baldwin, James, *Go Tell It On the Mountain* (1963) Corgi.

Baraka, Amiri, *Selected Poetry* (1979) William Morrow & Co. Inc.

Bakhtin, Mikhail, *Rabelais and his World* (trans. Helene Iswolsky) (1968) MIT Press.

Bakhtin, Mikhail, 'The Ruin of a Poetics' (trans. V. Mylne), *Twentieth Century Studies*, 7/8.

Barthes, R., *Writing Degree Zero*, Hill Wang (1967).

Barthes, R., *Mythologies* (1957;) Paladin, 1973).

Barthes, R., *S/Z* (1975) Jonathan Cape.

Baugh, Edward (ed.), *Critics on Caribbean Literature* (1978)Allen & Unwin.

Bennett, Louise, *Jamaica Labrish* (1966) Sangsher.

Bennett, Tony, *'Text and History'* in Widdowson, *Re-reading English* (1982) Methuen.

Booth, Wayne C., 'Freedom of Interpretation: Bahktin and the Challenge of Feminist Criticism', in *Critical Inquiry* (1982) University of Chicago.

Bourdieu, P., 'Systems of Education and Systems of Thought', in Dale, R. *et al.* (1976).

Brathwaite, Kamau E., 'Timerhi' (1970) *Savacou 2*.

Brathwaite, Kamau E., *Arrivants* (1973) Oxford University Press.

Brathwaite, Kamau E., *Contradictory Omens: Cultural Diversity and Integration in the Caribbean* (1974) Savacou Publications.

Brathwaite, Kamau E., *Other Exiles* (1975) Oxford University Press.

Brathwaite, Kamau E., 'The Love Axe/1: Developing a Caribbean Aesthetic 1962-1974', in Baker (1976).

Brathwaite, Kamau E., ed. *Savacou* 14/15: *New Poets from Jamaica* (1979).

Brathwaite, Kamau E., *The History of the Voice* (1984) New Beacon Books.

Brathwaite, Kamau E., *X-Self* (1987) Oxford University Press.

Brice-Heath, Shirley, *Ways with Words* (1983) Cambridge University Press.

Brookner, Peter, 'Post-structuralism, Reading and the Crisis in English', in Widdowson (1982).

Brown, Lloyd W., *West Indian Poetry* (1984) Heinemann.

Cabral, Amilcar, *Revolution In Guinea* (1969) *Selected texts by Amilcar Cabral* – Stage 1.

Cabral, Amilcar, *Return to the Source: Selected Writings of Amilcar Cabral* (1973) Monthly Review Press.

Césaire, Aimé, *Return to my Native Land* (1956; Penguin 1969).

Césaire, Aimé, 'Princes and Powers', in James Baldwin, *Nobody Knows My Name* (1961) Dell Publishing.

Chinweizu, Onwucheckwa Jemie, Ihechukwu Madubuike, *Towards the Decolonization of African Literature* (1980) 4th Dimension Publications.

Christian, Barbara, *Black Feminist Criticism* (1985) Pergamon Press.

Coard, Bernard, *How the West Indian Child is Made Educationally Subnormal in the British School System* (1971) New Beacon Books.

Cooper, Carolyn, 'Proverb as Metaphor in the Poetry of Louise Bennett', *Jamaica Journal*, no.17, 1984.

Corcoron B. and Evans E. (eds.), *Readers, Texts and Teachers* (1987) Boynton/Cook Publishers Inc.

Croydon Black Parents Committee, *Education and Your Child* publ. Croydon Black Parents Committee (undated).

Culler, Jonathan, *On Deconstruction* (1983) Routledge & Kegan Paul.

Dale *et al. Schooling and Capitalism: A Sociological Reader* (1976) Routledge and Kegan Paul in Association with OUP.

Dabydeen, David, *Slave Song* (1984) Dangaroo Press.

Dabydeen, David, *The Black Presence in English Literature* (1985) Manchester University Press.

Dabydeen, David, *Coolie Odyssey* (1988) Hansib/Dangaroo Press.

Dalphinis, Morgan, *Caribbean and African Languages* (1985) Karia Press.

Davies, Tony, 'Education, Ideology and Literature', *Red Letters*, 7 (1980).

Derrida, Jacques, 'Signature, event, context', GLYPH 1 (1966) Johns Hopkins University Press.

Dhondy, F., Hassan, L. and Beese, B., 'The Black Explosion in British Schools', *Race Today* (1982).

Doyle, Brian, 'Against the Tyranny of the Past', *Red Letters*, 10 (1980).

Doyle, Brian, 'The Hidden History of English Studies', in Widdowson (1982).

Eagleton, Terry, *Literary Theory: An Introduction* (1983) Blackwell.

Eagleton, Terry, 'The Subject of Literature', *The English Magazine*, 15 (1985).

Evans, E., 'Readers Re-creating Texts', in Corcoron and Evans (eds) 1987.

Exton, Richard, 'The Post-Structuralist, Always Reads Twice!' *The English Magazine*, 10 (1982).

Fanon, Frantz, *Black Skins White Masks* (1952; Grove Press 1967).

Gates, Louis Jnr, *Black Literature and Literary Theory* (1984) Methuen.

Gilbert, Pam, 'Post Reader Response – The Deconstructive Critique' in Corcoran (1987).

Gilroy, P., 'Living Memory: An Interview with Toni Morrison', *City Limits*, (1988).

Gramsci, A., *Selection from the Prison Notebooks*, ed. Hoare and Nowell Smith (1971) Lawrence & Wishart.

Gramsci, A., 'The Intellectuals', in Dale *et al.* (1976).

Greene, Gayle and Khan, Coppélia, *Making a Difference: Feminist Literary Criticism* (1985) Methuen.

Gundara, Jagdish (ed.), *Racism Diversity and Education* (1986) Hodder and Stoughton.

Hall, S., 'Education and the Crisis of the Urban School' (1974) in Raynor, John and Harris, Elizabeth (eds), *Schooling in the City* (1977) Ward Lock Educational/Open University Press.

Hall, S., *Culture, Media, Language* (1980) Hutchinson.

Hall, S., 'Teaching Race', *Multiracial Education*, vol. 9, no. 1 (1980).

Hawkes, Terence, *Structuralism and Semiotics* (1985) Metheun.

Hymes, D.H., *On Communicative Competence* (1971) University of Pennsylvania Press.

Irele, Abiola, *The African Experience in Literature and Ideology* (1981) Heinemann.

Iyasere, Solomon Ogbede, 'African Critics on African Literature: a Study in Misplaced Hostility' in Jones (1975).

Jordan, June, *Civil Wars* (1981) Beacon Press.

Joans, Ted, 'You'd Better Believe It', in *Selected Poems*, ed. Paul Brennan (1973) Penguin.

Jones, Eldred Durosimi (ed.), *Focus On Criticism* African Literature Today: 7 (1975) Heinemann.

Jones, Eldred Durosimi (ed.), *Insiders and Outsiders* African Literature Today: 14 (1984) Heinemann.

Jones, Eldred Durosimi (ed.), *The Novel in Africa* African Literature Today: 5 (1973) Heinemann.

Kimberley, Keith, 'The School Curriculum', in Gundara, Jagdish (1986).

Kingman, Sir John (chair.), *Committee of Enquiry into the Teaching of English* (1988) H.M.S.O.

Labov, W., The Logic of Non-Standard English', in Dittmar, N. *Sociolinguistics* (1976) Penguin.

Lamming, George, *The Pleasures of Exile* (1960; Allison & Busby 1984).

Lamming, George, *In the Castle Of My Skin* (1953) Longman.

Leavis, F.R., *Mass Civilization, Minority Culture* (1930; Arden Library 1979).

Leavis, F.R. *Culture and Environment* (1933) Chatto & Windus.

Longhurst, Derek, *Producing a National Culture: Shakespeare in Education*, Red Letters 8 (1978).

Lorde, Audré, *The Black Unicorn* (1978) W.W. Norton and Company Inc. New York.

McKay, Claude, *A Long Way From Home* (1937; Pluto Press 1985).

McKay, Claude, *Banana Bottom* (1933; Pluto Press 1986).

Marshall, Paule, The Poets in the Kitchen', in *Merle and Other Stories* (1986) Virago.

Mercer, Colin, 'Culture and Ideology in Gramsci', *Red Letters*, 8 (1978).

Miller, Jane (ed.), *Eccentric Propositions* (1984) Routledge & Kegan Paul.

Morley, Dave, *Texts, Readers and Subjects* in Hall (1980).

Morrison, Toni, *Beloved* (1987) Chatto & Windus.

Naipaul, V. S., *Miguel St* (1959; Penguin 1971).

Naipaul, V. S., *The Mimic Men* (1967) Penguin.

Ngara, Emmanuel, *Art and Ideology in the African Novel* (1985) Heinemann.

Ngugi Wa Thiongo, *Writers Politics* Heinemann.

Ngui Wa Thiongo, *Decolonising The Mind* (1981) Heinemann.

Onoge, Onafume F., *Marxism and African Literature* (1985) James Curry.

O'Flinn, J.P., 'Towards A Sociology of the Nigerian Novel' in *Focus On Criticism* (1975) ed. E. Durosimi Jones.

Pollard, Velma, 'The Social History of Dread Talk', *Caribbean Quarterly* 28, no. 4, December 1982, University of the West Indies.

Ponorska, Krystyna, 'Mikhail Bakhtin and his Verbal Universe', *A Journal for Descriptive Poetics and Theory of Literature*, 3 (1978) North Holland.

Probst, Robert E., 'Dialogue with a Text', (1988) *English Journal*, 77.

Protherough, R., 'Stories that Readers Tell', in Corcoron and Evans (eds) 1987.

Rohlehr, Gordon, 'Sparrow and the Language of Calypso', *Savacou*, 2 (1968).

Rosen, Harold, *Neither Bleak House nor Liberty Hall* (1982) Institute of Education, University of London, Bedford Way Papers.

Said, Edward, *The World, the Text and the Critic* (1984) Faber & Faber.

Sampson, Anthony, Review of *A Wreath for Udomo*, *Observer* (1956).

Senghor, Leopold. S., in Baldwin, *Nobody Knows My Name* (1961) Dell Publishing.

Senghor, Leopold. S., *Prose and Poetry* (1965) OUP trans. John Reed and Clive Wake.

Smith, Barbara, 'Towards a Black Feminist Criticism', in *The New Feminist Criticism*, ed. E. Showalter (1986) Virago.

Smith, Barbara (ed.), *Home Girls* (1983) New York Kitchen Table Women of Colour Press.

Smith, Michael, 'Mi Cyaan Believe It' in *Savacou* 14/15; also on Island Records 1983.

Steiner, George, *Language and Silence: Essays on Language, Literature and the Inhuman* (1976) Atheneum.

Stone, Maureen, *The Education of the Black Child in Britain* (1981) Fontana.

Stuart, Andrea, 'Telling Our Story: An Interview with Toni Morrison', *Spare Rib*, April 1988.

Toomer, Jean, *Cane* (1923; Liveright, 1975).

Trudgill, Peter, *Sociolinguistics* (1983) Penguin.

Vygotsky, Lev Semenovitch, *Thought and Language* (1962) MIT Press.

Walker, Alice, *In Search of our Mother's Gardens* (1984) The Women's Press.

Warner, Keith, *The Trinidad Calypso: the study of calypso as oral literature* (1982) Heinemann.

Widdowson, P. (ed.) *Re-reading English* (1982) Methuen.

Williams, Raymond, *Culture and Society* (1958) Penguin.

Williams, Raymond, *The Long Revolution* (1971) Penguin.

Williams, Raymond, 'Base and Superstructure in Marxist Cultural Theory' in Dale *et al.* (1976).

Williams, Raymond, *Marxism and Literature* (1977) Oxford University Press.

Willis, Susan, 'Black Women Writers' in Green and Khan (1985).

Wright, Edgar (ed.), *The Critical Evaluation of African Literature* (1973) Heinemann.

Index

THE EDUCATION SERIES
In association with the University of London Institute of Education
Series Editor JANE MILLER

In recent years the attacks on education in Britain have meant a complete redrawing of the educational map. But attempts to stifle opposition and resistance have neither silenced nor deterred those who are doing innovatory work in every aspect of the field. In support of this radical tradition, Virago has launched a new education series, published in association with the University of London Institute of Education, committed to providing information and understanding of the social, cultural and developmental issues of significance in education today. It presents some of the most exciting and important thinking in ways which will appeal to professionals as well as to students and parents and all those for whom education is a central and continuing concern. The books are by teachers and researchers and originate from classrooms in schools and colleges, from the practices of teaching and the experiences of learning. The series' general editor is Jane Miller, Senior Lecturer in the Joint Department of English and Media Studies at the Institute of Education. The first three launch titles are: COUNTING GIRLS OUT by The Girls and Mathematics Unit, Institute of Education, compiled by Valerie Walkerdine; TEACHING BLACK LITERATURE by Suzanne Scafe and UN/POPULAR FICTIONS by Gemma Moss.

COUNTING GIRLS OUT
Girls and Mathematics Unit, Institute of Education

Compiled by Valerie Walkerdine

The question of girls' attainment in mathematics is met with every kind of myth, false 'evidence', and theorising about the gendered body and the gendered mind. The Girls and Mathematics Unit has, over a period of ten years, carried out detailed theoretical and empirical investigations in this area. In taking issue with truisms such as: women are irrational, illogical and too close to their emotions to be any good at mathematics, this study examines and puts into historical perspective claims made about women's minds. It analyses the relationship between evidence and explanation: why are girls still taken to be lacking when they perform well, and boys taken to possess something even when they perform poorly? *Counting Girls Out* is an enquiry into the bases of these assumptions; it contains examples of work carried out with girls, their teachers and their families – at home and in the classroom – and discusses the problems and possibilities of feminist research more generally.

UN/POPULAR FICTIONS

Gemma Moss

Many young people take popular fiction as the model for their own writing. Yet little has been done to account for the preponderance of such forms or the function they fulfil for their writers. Concentrating on girls' use of romance, Gemma Moss shows that they are not mindlessly enslaved to the forms they reproduce, but are actively deploying them to raise rich and complex questions about social identity. She suggests that by drawing attention to the contradictions between the different sets of knowledge children use in their writing, questions about power and questions about difference, about masculinity and femininity can be raised. *Un/Popular Fictions* examines the conflicting assumptions made about the role of texts in the social development of children, suggests new strategies for classroom teaching, and offers new insights into the ways in which cultural identities are negotiated.

Announcing two new Education Series titles to be published in Spring 1990:

WASTING GIRLS' TIME
The Problem of Home Economics

Dena Attar

Wasting Girls' Time, a critical examination of the history and current status of domestic subjects in schools, looks at why and how these subjects were first included in school curricula, their subsequent effect on girls' education as a whole, and what feminist opposition to them has been. It also focuses on the struggles of domestic science pioneers and their modern counterparts to defend, upgrade and modernise their subject in spite of their low status, and the subject's identity as the domain of girls and women. It explores where boys fit in, what courses they are offered, how their attitudes differ and whether domestic subjects should be taught to both sexes. Using contemporary teaching materials, syllabuses and classroom observations, this informative study provides a detailed picture of home economics in schools now, and questions whether this subject has had its day or not.

READ IT TO ME, NOW!
Learning at Home and at School

Hilary Minns

Read it to me, Now! is a book about five four-year-olds who will all become pupils at the same primary school. It covers both the pre-school period, focussing on the children's backgrounds and their experience of reading and writing, and the first few months of school – their developing awareness of themselves as readers and writers. Hilary Minns points out that children do not arrive at school as 'non-readers', but as having unique reading histories of their own, learnt socially and culturally within their family and community. There is Gemma, from a working-class family, who, at first unused to handling books in the home, slowly changes literacy practices in the family; Gurdeep, arriving at school with a rich knowledge of sacred Sikh tales his mother heard as a girl in India; Anthony, already with a highly developed sense of narrative, learnt mainly from stories and TV dramas; Geeta, who took herself seriously as a reader long before she came to school; and Reid, arriving at school with the feeling that reading was something easily achieved. In drawing together these stories, Hilary Minns illuminatingly suggests ways towards the creation of a total literacy environment for children while recognising the individual character of each child's reading history.

Other Virago Books of Interest:

DEMOCRACY IN THE KITCHEN
Regulating Mothers and Socialising Daughters

Valerie Walkerdine and Helen Lucey

How are daughters raised, how are mothers made to be 'proper' mothers, and what does all this have to do with democracy? From the post-war period, with its emphasis on expanding educational possibilities for all children, to equal opportunities in the 1970s and '80s, the prevailing notion has been that 'natural' mothering (for how could it be otherwise?) would produce 'normal' children, fit for the new democratic age. These ideas have become commonsense ones, but at what cost to the lives of women? Valerie Walkerdine and Helen Lucey explore these effects by examining a well-known study of four-year-olds with their mothers, and in doing so, they tell us a different story about the divides of class and gender and the consequent social inequalities. The authors argue that although ideas from developmental psychology are held to be progressive, they serve to support the view that there is something wrong with working-class mothering which could be put right by making it more middle-class. But nor is the middle-class home one of happy normality: in both classes, women are differently, but oppressively, regulated. In this provocative book, the authors call for a new feminist engagement with class and gender socialisation to constitute a new politics of difference.

THE HEART OF THE RACE
Black Women's Lives in Britain

Beverley Bryan, Stella Dadzie and Suzanne Scafe

Winner of the Martin Luther King Memorial Prize 1985

'A balanced tribute to the undefeated creativity, resilience and resourcefulness of Black women in Britain today' – Margaret Busby, *New Society*

'A long overdue opportunity to set the record straight . . . a considerable achievement' – Brenda Polan, *Guardian*

'Our aim has been to tell it as we know it, placing our story within its history at the heart of our race, and using our own voices and lives to document the day-to-day realities of Afro-Caribbean women in Britain over the past forty years.'

The Heart of the Race powerfully records what life is like for Black women in Britain: grandmothers drawn to the promise of the 'mother country' in the 1950s talk of a different reality; young girls describe how their aspirations at school are largely ignored; working women tell of their commitments to families, jobs, communities. With clarity and determination, these Afro-Caribbean women discuss their treatment by the Welfare State, their housing situations, their health, their self-images – and their confrontation with the racism they encounter all too often. Here too is Black women's celebration of their culture and their struggle to create a new social order in this country.

THE TIDY HOUSE
Little Girls' Writing

Carolyn Steedman

Three working-class eight-year-old girls write a story, 'The Tidy House'. It is about the house they will live in one day, the streets of their own decaying urban estate, about love and motherhood and the pattern of life they expect to inherit. The children in the story are themselves as they believe their parents see them – longed for, yet because of poverty, also sources of irritation and resentment.

In analysing this fascinating document, the author uses her remarkable perceptions of children's writing and their expectations of the world, as well as literature, linguistics, theories of education and history, to come to her highly original and controversial conclusions on how children confront the way things are and imagine the way things might be.

'. . . very interesting and heartening. Seeing the problems and rewards of children's perceptions and writings that close is a great help to understanding a much wider and more persistent process' – *Raymond Williams*

'. . . a revelation – superbly constructed and illuminating. Opens up new ways of looking at the way children learn' – *Dale Spender*